NEW ENGLAND UFOs

NEW ENGLAND UFOs

Sightings, Abductions, and Other Strange Phenomena

TARYN PLUMB

Down East Books
Guilford, Connecticut

Published by Down East Books
An imprint of Globe Pequot
Trade division of The Rowman & Littlefield Publishing Group, Inc.
4501 Forbes Blvd., Ste. 200
Lanham, MD 20706
www.rowman.com
www.downeastbooks.com

Distributed by NATIONAL BOOK NETWORK

British Library Cataloguing in Publication Information available

Library of Congress Cataloging-in-Publication Data available

Names: Plumb, Taryn, 1981– author.
Title: New England UFOs : sightings, abductions, and other strange phenomena
   / Taryn Plumb.
Description: Lanham, MD : Down East Books, [2019] | Includes bibliographical
   references.
Identifiers: LCCN 2019002603 (print) | LCCN 2019004049 (ebook) | ISBN
   9781608936700 (Electronic) | ISBN 9781608936694 (pbk. : alk. paper)
Subjects: LCSH: Unidentified flying objects—Sightings and encounters—New
   England. | Human-alien encounters—New England. | Alien abduction—New
   England.
Classification: LCC TL789.5.N6 (ebook) | LCC TL789.5.N6 .P58 2019 (print) |
   DDC 001.9420974—dc23
LC record available at https://lccn.loc.gov/2019002603

∞™ The paper used in this publication meets the minimum requirements of American National Standard for Information Sciences—Permanence of Paper for Printed Library Materials, ANSI/ NISO Z39.48-1992.

Printed in the United States of America

"L: Oh, my Carmen, my little Carmen . . . I remember those sultry nights. And the stars and the cars and the bars and the barmen . . .

H: And the bars that sparkled and the cars that parkled . . . And the curs that barkled and the birds that larkled . . .

L: And oh my charmin', our dreadful fights . . .

H: Such dreadful blights . . ."

Contents

CONTENTS

CONTENTS

Introduction

So long as humans have had the ability and the where-withal to look up—which is to say, almost always—we have.

Our earliest methods of charting time and place were based on the paths and patterns of our own sun and the far more distant stars. Once we had gods to revere and worship, we created constellations honoring them, playing out their origin stories and exploits. Our very perception of heaven came to mean looking skyward.

Always inventing and tinkering, we created looking glasses to get a glimpse of what might be visible beyond our simple human vision. We mapped our own solar system; created stronger, bigger, and more powerful scopes; probed deeper and deeper into the still-untapped, fathomless reaches of space.

Since achieving once-impossible notions of manned space flight and moon landings (deniers duly noted), we established a long-term habitable International Space Station; launched the Mars Rover; and sent Voyagers, the Hubble Space Telescope, and other advanced observatories and mechanical explorers into even further depths of outer space.

To ring in the new year 2019, the National Aeronautics and Space Administration (NASA) made an announcement that could change our very understanding of our solar system. Its New Horizons interplanetary space probe, launched in 2006, made a landmark flyby of a billions-year-old fossil floating in the Kuiper belt, a collection of icy rocks surrounding the periphery of our solar system. Ultima Thule, known scientifically as 2014 MU69, has become the most distant planetary object humans have ever flown by. (Its name is derived from ancient Greek and Roman literature and cartography, "Thule" marking the farthest-north location). What's more, researchers hope the contact with this ancient artifact will someday provide crucial insights into the very makeup, formation, and history of our solar system.

Bit by bit, we continue to expand our knowledge of what lies beyond the ether.

Still, there are many more unknowns than knowns—since time immemorial, we've considered the possibility of life elsewhere in our solar system and distant galaxies. It was the great Carl Sagan who put into words what an "awful waste of space" it would be if God created the entirety of the universe just for us.

The term "Martians" has become ubiquitous; theories have cropped up that link "ancient aliens" to the enigmas of the pyramids and Stonehenge; endless stories and legends venture to guess what other beings might look, live, and act like.

And then in 1947 came the bizarre crashing of a weather balloon at Roswell, an incident that spawned the widespread notion of flying saucers and UFOs (the uppercase, out-of-this-world kind) and that has since become synonymous with government conspiracies, cover-ups, and "men in black" theories. While the government confirmed that it was a nuclear test balloon, conspiratorial types spread the idea that it had been an alien ship—and that an extraterrestrial being had even been recovered from it. (This was later accompanied by an infamous "alien autopsy" video that the filmmaker Spyros Melaris eventually conceded was a fake.)

Reports of flying saucers and even encounters with "little gray men" began to skyrocket (forgive the pun). Books, movies, and television shows were replete with science fiction stories. The pseudoscience of ufology was born; it was taken up by, among many others, the likes of Raymond E. Fowler, a Salem, Massachusetts, native who authored books on all the most notorious New England abduction cases, and J. Allen Hynek, an astronomer, consultant to Project Blue Book, and founder of the Center for UFO Studies.

The federal government launched first Project Sign, then Project Grudge, and finally Project Blue Book to determine if UFOs were a threat to national security and to scientifically analyze UFO-related data. From 1947 to 1969, Project Blue Book investigated 12,618 sightings. Of those, just 701 were deemed of "unidentified" origin, while 11, 917 were found to have been caused by misinterpretation of material objects, such as balloons, satellites, and aircraft; immaterial occurrences, including lightning, weather phenomenon, reflections, and refractions; astronomical bodies, such as stars, planets, meteors, the sun, and the moon; man-made explosives, fireworks, and lanterns; not to mention outright hoaxes and attention-seekers.

The program was officially shut down in December 1969, its documents declassified, and the government stated: (1) No UFO reported, investigated, and evaluated by the US Air Force was ever an indication of threat to our national security; (2) There was no evidence submitted to or discovered by the US Air Force that sightings categorized as "unidentified" represented technological developments or principles beyond the range of modern scientific knowledge; and (3) There was no evidence indicating that sightings categorized as "unidentified" were extraterrestrial vehicles.

Despite this dismantling of Project Blue Book before the dawning of the 1970s, sightings certainly didn't cease—nor did reports, although it would take some claimants until the internet age to have the opportunity to share them with an audience.

In this era beyond the fantasy of *2001: A Space Odyssey*—where *The X-Files*, *Star Trek*, *Star Wars* (in all their iterations), *Men in Black*, and phrases like "The truth is out there" and "Space: The Final Frontier" are popular culture mainstays—groups such as the Mutual UFO Network (MUFON) and the National Investigations Committee on Aerial Phenomena (NICAP) independently investigate sightings and examine evidence. Meanwhile, numerous websites, most prominently the National UFO Reporting Center (NUFORC), allow would-be witnesses to share their encounters. And today you can even test your odds of seeing a UFO on Casino.org. (Brave new world, indeed.)

Project Blue Book files were made widely available to the public through online archives in 2015; a new eponymous drama series on the History Channel explores the "authentic historic events" behind them. In December 2018 the *New York Times* reported a bombshell that reinforced long-held notions of conspiracy theorists: Between 2007 and 2012, the Senate authorized $22 million for a secret Pentagon initiative known as the Advanced Aerospace Threat Identification Program. Funded at the request of Nevada Democrat Harry Reid, it explored sightings of aircraft that seemed to move at high velocities with no visible signs of propulsion or that hovered with no apparent means to lift, according to the *Times*. Some insiders claim that this shadowy program still exists.

In this book we look at the history of UFO encounters in New England, from the notorious Betty and Barney Hill abductions in New Hampshire, to the Allagash abductions in Maine, to numerous other lesser-known occurrences.

But first, a word about "UFOs": The term was coined in the 1950s by the US Air Force to describe "any airborne object which by performance, aerodynamic characteristics, or unusual features does not conform to any presently known aircraft or missile type, or which cannot be positively identified as a familiar object." In pithier context, it's anything in the sky that can't be identified (which, ultimately, means that we've all seen one at some time or another). Researchers report that 99.9 percent of what is seen in the sky can be attributed to objects created and sent aloft by man, generated by atmospheric conditions, or caused by celestial bodies or the residue of meteoric activity.

Still, there remains that 0.1 percent.

ONE

MASSACHUSETTS

Mysterious History

The universe is under no obligation to make sense to you.
—Neil deGrasse Tyson

They gave off a feeling of love and of warmth—there was really no other way to describe it. The beings, "the elders" as she came to know them, transported her to places beyond our earthly dimensions, places bathed in both welcoming light and endless mystery. These creatures were in turn guided by a greater entity described all-encompassingly as "the one," whom she had met and interacted with but was sworn never to speak of in any depth.

For years, beginning when she was a child, they visited her, kept track of her, reminded her that there was something wonderful beyond the confines of her benign, everyday life.

So claimed Betty Andreasson, a housewife from the tiny town of South Ashburnham in north-central Massachusetts. Her accounts of a lifelong relationship with otherworldly beings is one of the most vivid and extensively detailed, ongoing alien abduction scenarios in history.

1

Andreasson's story burns bright in the vibrant constellation of Massachusetts stories involving the unknown and the unexplained.

Thousands upon thousands of encounters have been reported across the earliest-settled, historically rich, densely populated central heart of New England. The Bay State is, in fact, the location of the country's first reported UFO sighting, the highly contested landing pad of the first monument recognizing off-world craft—and even, some say, where bona fide proof was captured on mainstream celluloid (in *Jaws*, which was filmed on Martha's Vineyard).

Ultimately, Massachusetts is full of history and mystery—big, small, and immeasurable.

A NEW WORLD INDEED

Almost as soon as the Pilgrims took their first fateful, cautious steps onto the shores of the savage, uncharted "new world," they began to report strange phenomena.

John Winthrop, governor of the Massachusetts Bay Colony, dutifully and prolifically recorded them just as he did the banalities, calamities, and victories of the colonists.

On the first day of March 1639, he set down a curious encounter relayed to him by James Everell, an otherwise "sober and discreet" man.

Everell and two others had been rowing along the Muddy River—which today runs through Boston's Emerald Necklace Conservatory before emptying into the Charles River—when a bright, fiery light materialized in the sky before them. Willowy and shapeshifting, "when it stood still, it flamed up, and was about three yards square," the governor reported. Whereas, "when it ran, it was contracted into the figure of a swine." (Yes, you read that right: a pig.)

The three boatmen watched the shapeshifting light, enthralled, for two or three hours, during which it "ran as swift as an arrow," darting back and forth between the river area and the village of Charlestown about two miles away.

The trio also reported that they had lost time—a condition that would become common in the abductee narrative.

After the shock of seeing the strange lights began to dull, they found themselves "carried quite back against the tide" about a mile upstream. But with memories as foggy as the night, they had no recollection whatsoever of paddling the distance. It was almost as if, they said, the light had transported them there.

Many have since speculated about this first-reported account: They were nudged along by the wind or a reverse tidal flow. And the shifting glow? It was the ignis fatuus phenomenon, or a pale light resulting in marshy areas from the breakdown of organic matter (in other words, swamp gas).

James Savage, writing in an 1825 edition of Winthrop's journal that he compiled, added a footnote to this effect. "This account of an ignis fatuus may easily be believed on testimony less respectable than that which was adduced," he theorized. "Some operation of the devil, or other power beyond the customary agents of nature, was probably imagined by the relaters and hearers of that age, and the wonder of being carried a mile against the tide became important corroboration of the imagination."

He concluded that "perhaps they were wafted during the two or three hours' astonishment . . . by the wind; but, if this suggestion be rejected, we might suppose, that the eddy [whirlpool], flowing always, in our rivers, contrary to the tide in the channel, rather than the meteor, carried their lighter back."

Ultimately, though, because they were prudent and well respected—and they lived in a time when superstitions and otherworldly phenomena were, if not wholeheartedly accepted, more roundly received and in some cases heeded—their story was believed. Winthrop also backed up their account by adding that "diverse other credible persons saw the same light, after, about the same place."

Nearly five years later, in January 1644, the governor set down another series of peculiar encounters. These started on January 18, when a group of men rowing along Boston Harbor suddenly spotted lights arising from the water; these lights quickly assumed the form of a man, sailed "leisurely" over the harbor, then vanished.

A week later these strange lights were seen again, this time by many. Some viewers reported that at around 8:00 p.m., one light "resembling the moon" rose from the water, traveled a short ways, and was met by its twin light; the two then repeatedly merged and parted, in a seemingly playful manner, "shooting out sometimes flames and sometimes sparkles." The pair finally united into one luminous disc and disappeared.

Meanwhile, another group of witnesses a little north along the harbor reported a disembodied voice moving around above the water and crying out, "Boy! Boy! Come away! Come away!" It was heard about 20 times "by divers[e] Godly persons," Winthrop wrote.

In this instance, he had an explanation (of sorts). Both spectacles had occurred near the location where a ship had exploded and sunk a few weeks earlier—the result, he related, of an accidental lighting of gunpowder that killed five sailors. All but one of the bodies was recovered; the one outstanding was believed to have been responsible for the tragedy—a sailor who professed the ability to communicate with the dead. It was chocked up, then, to the devil's work.

Some have since called this the first reported instance of the rare USO, or "unidentified submerged object"—basically an aquatic UFO—in American history.

Of course as the settlers expanded their population and territory, strange experiences continued. In one account, from August 1765, witnesses were captivated and alarmed by a "flying black giant" approximating the size and shape of a human body, as documented in the *Boston Gazette*, one of the first pre–Revolutionary War newspapers. Hovering over Boston, it remained until sunset and was reportedly seen by thousands. They watched, it was said, as the entity touched down, alighted, flopped, and swelled. Floating about 20 feet off the ground, it let forth vapor smoke and sparks, grew "excessively black and fierce," and boomed thunder that tore down at least one building and "shook the lofty fabric and all the little houses, and hollow hearts did hear it." After more than four hours of this relentless, ferocious behavior, it suddenly vanished, leaving behind abrupt tranquility and silence.

Similarly, in April 1778, a multitude of witnesses from Boston to southern New Hampshire were astounded to see a black cloud striding a few feet above the ground, described as moving at the speed of a galloping horse. Passing unperturbed through walls and fences "as one goes through water," it set forth the continual shriek of "Hoo! Hoo!" The shock, apparently, caused some onlookers to faint helplessly.

The first known report of the twentieth century occurred over Worcester (smack in the middle of the state). On December 22, 1909, according to both the *New-York Tribune* and the *New York Sun*, a "mysterious airship" emitting a bright beam of light appeared moving southeast to northwest, hovering above the city before moving away. It was seen once more two hours later, bobbing in the sky slightly before moving away to the southeast. The next night, the papers reported, it (or something like it) was seen again over Boston and its suburb of Lynn.

We can only wonder: Were these "presences" evidence of something much more ancient and long-lingering—or, right along with our own explorers, were they, too, plumbing and probing the depths of a newly discovered world?

JAW-DROPPING EVIDENCE?

Jaws is an icon of cinema that started out as a massive sleeper hit in 1975 (establishing Steven Spielberg as a directorial dynamo; coincidentally or not, his follow-up was the 1977 masterpiece and multiple Oscar winner *Close Encounters of the Third Kind*). But some say the story of the voracious, insatiable killer shark originally thought up by author Peter Benchley also bears evidence of UFOs.

The movie was primarily filmed on and off the waters of the fishing village of Menemsha on Martha's Vineyard.

After years of inspection and dissection, UFO enthusiasts point to several frames in the film shot while actors Roy Scheider (Chief Brody), Richard Dreyfuss (Matt Hooper), and Robert Shaw (Quint) are out hunting the man-eating great white. After the three men reminisce and sing "Show Me the Way to Go Home" and the shark finally shows up, literally chewing the scenery, the men run outside onto the deck. A white streak appears behind Brody's head, moving from top right to lower left. In ensuing frames, another bright light can be seen whizzing by from right to left. Finally, as the *Orca* drifts in the hazy twilight, two dark specks can be seen hovering above the horizon.

Spielberg acknowledged in later interviews that he placed shooting stars in his movies as an homage to his father, whose night out watching a meteor shower with his future Hollywood bigwig son in part inspired *Close Encounters*. Still, he says this wasn't the case with *Jaws*. He was too concerned with wrangling the malfunctioning mechanical shark.

Others say the unknown objects are indeed shooting stars or meteors, specifically the Perseids. Still more say they are merely dust particles or specks on the film itself.

Many, though, aren't convinced, and the matter is still debated and analyzed.

In any case, it makes one wonder: What would *The Twilight Zone–Jaws* theme mash-up sound like?

THE BIZARRE CASE OF THE ROVING UFO

It landed—lingered—took off—then landed once more.

The monument, that is.

You'd be forgiven if you thought we were talking about a UFO. In this long, strange (and ongoing) saga, the purported flying saucer that triggered everything is really just part of the story.

In 2015 the Great Barrington Historical Society and Museum issued a highly unusual citation (that is, in contrast to the expected dry and dusty declarations commemorating native tribes, town elders, landmarks, and homesteads). Dated February 6, it honored an infamous UFO event that was witnessed in the town of Sheffield and four surrounding towns on September 1, 1969. The widely reported "off-world incident" was "historically significant and true," according to the society, and would be included in its historic archives.

Accompanying this was an official citation from Governor Charlie Baker, noting a "dedicated service" to the incident by locals that was "factually upheld, founded, and deemed historically significant and true by means of Massachusetts Historians."

The out-of-this-world proclamations, believed to be the first of their kind, were set down to coincide with the erection of a privately funded memorial. The 6-foot-tall, 5,000-pound white monument was installed on what was believed to be private land in the town of Sheffield, adjacent to a replica of a nineteenth-century covered bridge. (Crossing the Housatonic River, the original bridge had burned in 1994.)

At first it was all fanfare—a quirky news story that was picked up by increasingly larger news outlets and shared in "Hey, Martha!" style. Debbie Opperman, director of the Great Barrington Historical Society, told the *Boston Globe* that the society's decision was not a unanimous one; some members were "strongly opposed." She lightheartedly acknowledged, "I know we're going to get a lot of backlash. We're going to get hammered. But we have given it an awful lot of thought, and, based on the evidence we've been given, we believe this is a significant and true event."

She added proudly that it was "the first time a mainstream historical society or museum in the United States has declared a UFO encounter to be historical fact."

The monument went up with the town's and society's (brief) blessings—not to mention that of the owner of Pine Island Farm, Louis Aragi. Dedicated to the late Dr. Howard W. Reed, Matthew R. Reed, and Nancy A. Reed—relatives of Thom Reed, one of the numerous witnesses of the 1969 event and greatest champion of the monument's installation—it is emblazoned on one side with the Massachusetts seal and a bronzed replica of the governor's citation and on the other with a plaque reading,

The Official Induction of our Nation's First Off-World/UFO Incident.

Whereas: The incident that occurred at this location, September 1st 1969 has been confirmed historically significant and true by means of factual corroborated evidence through the GT Barrington Historical Society.

MASSACHUSETTS

Whereas: Thomas E. Reed born 02-12-1960 and his families [sic] incident of Sept 1st 1969 has been recorded and formally inducted into the history of the commonwealth of Massachusetts on this day February 6th 2015.

Quote: "History is a story about the past that is significant and true. Yours is one of those amazing stories that we seek to share with our community." GBHS

In news articles immediately following its dedication, Thom Reed called the monument a "triumph in so many ways." "We're honored to have made such a mainstream contribution to this field," he said, noting that the event had started as a "community encounter" and "will remain a well-supported community encounter."

Well—in another world, maybe.

In a matter of weeks, the memorial was defaced with graffiti, and locals began to complain that it detracted from the historic tranquility of the covered bridge. Town officials revisited land maps and discovered that the celebratory monument to the otherworldly had been placed on a town-owned right-of-way.

The historical society and the state rapidly backed away. Opperman told the *Globe* in a follow-up story that the decision was "a mistake" and "a professional embarrassment." Similarly, a spokesperson for the governor's office said the citation of the "off-world incident" was "issued in error" (prompting journalists to question what else Baker might have mistakenly proclaimed).

The marker was moved 30 feet, remaining (or so, once again, it was believed) on Aragi's Pine Island Farm. In 2017 benches and solar lampposts were added—sponsored by the Reed family; the

International UFO Museum Research Center in Roswell, New Mexico; Ben Hansen of the Syfy TV show *Fact or Faked: Paranormal Files*; and author Travis Walton—creating a small and not-unpleasant grotto.

In the ongoing case of the unidentified shrinking parcel, the town came back once again in April 2018, claiming that the giant marker still remained on a town-owned easement (per an updated land survey). Officials ordered it to be removed. The matter moved to the courts—a far more tangled system, it can be assumed, than anything beyond the reaches of space.

But what of the UFO itself? The fact that a strange presence was detected in the skies by dozens of people has nearly been lost among the hubbub.

Reed—who, it should be noted, claimed a series of encounters as a child, beginning when he was six—was the principal witness. Age nine on that night in September 1969, he recalled riding home in a station wagon with his mother, grandmother, and brother.

While crossing the bridge, they looked back to see a "self-contained glow" moving along through the trees, he claimed. Once their car was back out on the open dirt road, it was flooded in amber light. The vehicle stopped; the barometric pressure seemed to shift; everything suddenly became very calm, slowed down, and silent, Reed claimed. He remembered the lights flickering through the trees, he told the *Berkshire Eagle*—and then the distinct sensation that they just weren't in the car anymore. Where they were, he didn't know; he described brief memories of something like a hangar crowded with people and glimpses of creatures that resembled ants with football-shaped heads.

But he recalled little else until he was back in the station wagon—where, curiously, his mother and grandmother had switched seats and purportedly more than two hours had passed.

Over the course of the night, 40 people from Sheffield, Great Barrington, Stockbridge, and South Egremont came forward with sightings, and local radio station WSBS took calls from witnesses describing the odd, ethereal lights.

"They didn't know it was a UFO at the time," station general manager David Isy later told WGBH. "They just called the station and said, 'Something bizarre is happening.'"

Among the captivated onlookers was Tom Warner; he was lying out on the ground in a field when suddenly "there was a beam on me," he recalled. What was it emanating from? Something "20 feet or more in height, probably about 30 to 40 feet around, and it had lights. . . . [They] were colors I'd never seen in my life."

"When you see something, it's like—I see you. I see that rock. I see that building," he said to reporters. "I *saw* that UFO."

This may be one of the rare instances where the unidentified craft is self-explanatory. The events surrounding the monument, though? That's the baffling part.

OTHERWORLDLY LIGHT, LOVE

Unlike the harrowing, probing, violating alien abduction accounts that have become the relative norm—if such a word can be used to describe them—Betty Andreasson Luca came to almost look forward to her ongoing, enlightening encounters with beings not of this world. The practicing Christian took them at first to be divinely influenced, only later exploring the notion of aliens and UFOs. But whatever the cause, they were unquestionably life-altering.

They began as early as 1944 when she was very young; these formative experiences were always brief, and she didn't recall ever being transported anywhere.

Then from 1950 she carried a potent memory of being outside one night and looking up at what she thought was the moon. Only, she began to realize, "it was getting bigger and bigger and seemed to be coming toward me." Decades later, while under regressive hypnosis, she would excavate memories of being taken aboard the craft, where the beings inserted a BB-sized tracking device into her head.

The event that eventually served as a tractor beam for ufologists, though, occurred in 1967.

It was just after dinner on January 25; Betty was at home in South Ashburnham with her mother, father, and seven children. The house lights suddenly winked out and came back on again. Nothing terribly out of the ordinary—but then a pulsating reddish-orange light shone in through the kitchen window.

Betty tried to calm the children as her father investigated. He was alarmed—there were, he claimed, very peculiar creatures hopping along toward the house.

They continued to approach, coming into the house by passing through the door as if it (or they, or both) were transparent. They immediately established a telepathic link with Betty and then placed the rest of the family in a state of suspended animation.

As Betty described later, the leader was roughly five feet tall; the others were about four feet tall. All of them had gray skin; three-fingered hands; and large, pear-shaped heads. Their ears and noses were tiny, their eyes "catlike" and "wraparound," and their mouths immobile slits that reminded Betty of scar lines. They wore boots and matching blue coveralls featuring an insignia of some kind of bird. They "levitated in a smooth fashion" rather than walked.

Naturally, Betty was frightened—but that fear was soon replaced by an overwhelming sense of friendship and camaraderie, she recalled. Sensing her concern for her family, the beings temporarily released her 11-year-old daughter, Becky, from her suspended state to assure her mother that she was all right.

"They gave off a feeling of love, and even though they moved about very methodically, and looked very odd, it felt [that] what was happening was supposed to be," Betty reflected years later.

While one being remained behind to keep watch, the housewife was ferried outside to a small craft that she described as being about 20 feet in diameter, pulsing with orange-red lights, and resembling two inverted saucers with a kind of "superstructure" at its top.

It lifted, took off, accelerated, and seemed to merge with a larger "parent" craft—a red-glowing environment full of tracks, tunnels, and cavernous hollows.

While aboard, the human ward was changed into a white garment and subjected to testing, she claimed, which included being wholly submerged in liquid while seated in a chair. The beings also removed the BB-like tracking device they had implanted years earlier, pulling it out of her nostril.

Several hours later, after 10:30 p.m., Betty was returned home, where her family remained in their peculiar state of suspension.

The visitors led them all to bed, then left.

Several times, Betty recalled, she had been told that the experiences would be locked in her mind until "the appointed time." As it happens, that time seemed to come in 1975, when she responded to a story in a local newspaper about UFO researcher Allen Hynek. The well-regarded investigator was soliciting personal accounts from the public. She sent in an outline of her experiences, although it was apparently so scant that there was no follow-up for several months.

In January 1977 she was finally contacted by researchers, who spent 12 months doing an extensive study. Their team consisted of not only a UFO investigator but also a professional hypnotist, a medical doctor trained in psychiatry, a solar physicist, electronics and aerospace engineers, and a telecommunications specialist.

Through numerous hypnosis sessions, she was brought back to the 1967 "abduction," as well as several other claimed encounters from her childhood.

Consistently, she referred to the creatures that had visited her family as "the grays"; they in turn had a symbiotic relationship with beings she called "the elders," whose leader she came to know as "Quazgaa." The elders were strikingly human-looking, with pale skin and blond, near-white hair. The significant difference was their height: They were at least seven feet tall. Their long, nimble frames were cloaked in white, billowy robes.

All of Betty's communication with both the grays and the elders was telepathic. Once, when she asked the latter who they were, they called themselves "masters of rings, cycles, and orbs" and ambassadors of a being named "Oh."

And Oh was? "The internal, external, eternal presence," they informed her.

When she was taken by the grays, it was usually to a mysterious location that seemed to be underground or close to the inner core of the Earth, she claimed. The elders, meanwhile, commanded a domain that was much grander and far off in the cosmos; willowy, full of light and shifting shapes, transformative and dynamic, it was much more up to interpretation.

In one regressive experience, Betty described seeing several versions of herself. "I came out of myself," she said while hypnotized. "I was just standing over there, and I was standing over here. There were two of me!"

She then described being guided to a "bright, really bright" wall of glass with a "big, big, big, big, big door." She was instructed to go through it and not to fear. She was going to meet "the one."

Although at this point her recollections became vague when prodded by the hypnotist, a rapturous smile crossed her face and she proclaimed that "love is the answer" and "everything fits together. Everything is one. It's beautiful!"

In other sessions she described watching what seemed to be ritualized acts of magic: Six elders stepped into a circle subdivided into six equal parts, touched their hands together, and produced beams of light from their foreheads. Those beams formed a perfect hexagram before merging and morphing into a beachball-sized sphere of lavender-purple light that was then plucked from the air and placed delicately onto a four-pronged stand.

On another occasion she was taken to an unidentifiable forest, where the elders interacted with kindly hobos, gifting them with glowing balls of light. She was also transported to the bedside of an old man dying in the hospital, where she witnessed a light-being and two entities of darkness tugging back and forth at him (presumably vying for his soul).

Then there was an overwhelming experience involving "the one": Betty, an elder, and a gray all became light-beings—golden, pure white, and light blue, respectively.

"I'm just engulfed in light and blending into that light," she described during hypnosis. "Oh! Oh, this is everything, everything, everything!"

Along with 14 extensive hypnosis sessions, Betty underwent two lie detector tests, a psychiatric interview, and character reference checks.

Ultimately, researchers found her accounts to be consistent, detailed, and producing genuine physiological reactions. In a lengthy report, they concluded that she was reliable and sane and sincerely believed the experiences had occurred.

Raymond E. Fowler, the godfather of UFO research, paired up with Betty and wrote several books on her experiences, including *The Andreasson Affair: The True Story of a Close Encounter of the Fourth Kind* (1980), *The Andreasson Affair Phase Two: The Continuing Investigation of a Woman's Abduction by Alien Beings* (1983), and *The Andreasson Legacy: UFOs and the Paranormal* (1997).

Through the years, despite scrutiny, support, some ridicule, and even outright hostility, Betty has held fast to her accounts and her beliefs—even though a so-called rational explanation has yet to present itself.

As she told *Alternative Perceptions Magazine*, "After all the experiences, exposure, and integration of this other dimension of reality, I feel more aware of life, its complexities, and how like a river it flows calmly onward."

BAFFLED IN BEVERLY

The 11-year-old's eyes grew wide.

What . . . was . . . THAT?

Lights had cast an arcing glow into her second-story bedroom window; because her house overlooked a busy intersection across from the high school, she thought maybe it was a car accident (which were frequent).

As she peered out, she did see something that was the size of a car—only it wasn't in the road below; it was floating in the air behind a big maple tree in the front yard, flashing blindingly bright lights in succession.

"I had no idea what it was," Nancy Coffey (née Modugno) told *Wicked Local Beverly* 50 years after the widely reported and mass-experienced event on April 22, 1966. "I think it was metallic and I remember the lights. I knew instantly that it was nothing I'd ever seen before."

She ran downstairs to tell her father—who, as it so happens, was banging on the family's TV, which had inexplicably gone out. Hoping to assuage the child, her mother and two neighbors clambered outside for a look.

The women were stupefied to see three giant objects maneuvering impossibly in the sky over the school's athletic fields. This was no child's imagination at work. Oval-shaped with bright flashing lights changing from red to green to blue (and back again), they started and stopped, circled, and turned in an almost playful manner.

One of the neighbors, Brenda Maria, waved her arms at them. Horrifyingly, the object that was closest stopped circling and began to move toward her.

"All I could see was a blurry atmosphere and brightly lit-up lights flashing slowly around. . . . I thought it might crash on my head!" she recalled. "The lights appeared to be all around and turning. The colors were very bright."

The other neighbor, Barbara Smith, likened it to "a giant mushroom" or "the bottom of a plate."

"I looked up and saw a round object," she remembered. "It was solid, grayish white. . . . I felt [that] this thing was going to come down on top of me."

It got about 20 feet above their heads before they turned and fled.

At that point, other neighbors had begun to come outside, alarmed by the large luminous objects flying around like something out of an Ed Wood movie. Someone phoned the police.

Officers arrived to find a crowd of people standing around in the street, gawking. At first they thought whatever had their attention was just an airplane—but then, suddenly, the thing turned bright red and dropped to a hover just above the school.

Identified only by their last names, Mahan and Bossie, the policemen described it as half-dollar-shaped, its three lights emanating from indentations at its rear. Mahan recalled that he "observed what seemed to be a large plate" bobbing above the school building; it made no noise whatsoever. Bossie, meanwhile, described how it "hovered and then began gliding," adding that "some of the people got on the ground and were real scared." The officers dove back in their cruiser and headed toward the object.

Coffey, her mother, and neighbors then realized that the two other craft had disappeared; the onlookers had apparently been too preoccupied with the closest one to notice. (That, or the craft had been too stealthy in their vanishing act.)

The remaining oval oddity made a couple of scans of the school grounds then picked up speed and flew out of sight. According to Coffey, some planes and helicopters then arrived on the scene.

In the days and weeks to come, many others in the north-of-Boston town would corroborate the appearance of the three bright, football-shaped bulks.

Soon the incident attracted the attention of Raymond Fowler, an investigator for the independent citizen group the National Investigations Committee on Aerial Phenomena (NICAP). Fowler performed numerous interviews and drew up sketches but ultimately came to no conclusions. He eventually passed his report on to the Condon Committee (a group from the University of Colorado contracted by the federal government to conduct UFO research).

In 1968 the committee published its landmark Condon report, assessing 59 cases involving purported UFO activity and providing rational explanations. The Beverly encounter was "Case #6," and the report listed "witness misidentification" as a possible explanation. Most likely, researchers concluded, it had been a particularly vibrant sighting of Jupiter.

However, the report assented, while the circumstance "did not yield impressive residual evidence, even in the narrative content," to support the hypothesis of an alien object or vehicle, it would "fit no other explanation if the testimony of the witnesses is taken at full value."

Coffey finds that last part telling. "I believe this is one of the cases where they really couldn't explain it away," she told *Wicked Local Beverly*. "It wasn't people seeking attention. We know what we saw."

She added that she wasn't the type of kid with a wild imagination who daydreamed or made up stories. In fact, she didn't even like science fiction, she said, and had never thought about UFOs before that April night.

Now, though? That's indubitably changed.

"I always look up. I guess I believe," she said. "Why wouldn't I believe? Why would we think we're the only planet in the universe with life on it?"

ALSO THAT YEAR . . .

1966 is widely regarded as a prolific year for UFO activity, with a flurry of phenomena reported across the country, even the world. Massachusetts wasn't excluded from that, of course: Sightings of various durations and magnitude were claimed by observers across the state, with several investigated by the federal government's Project Blue Book.

Among those was a case in Weston (just west of Boston) on two separate days in January, involving two quite different anomalies.

J. Allen Hynek, director of the Dearborn Observatory at Northwestern University, interviewed the witness—who, an abnormality in itself, is identified by name (in keeping with government protocol involving declassified files, observer identities have been blacked out throughout Project Blue Book reports). Perhaps this is because of Hynek's esteem for the witness, Roger Woodbury, an associate director of the instrumentation laboratory at the Massachusetts Institute of Technology (MIT). Hynek calls him a man whose "reliability as an observer and as a person of technical competence" could not be questioned.

In his first encounter, on January 14, Woodbury described an object that had a central white light of a "very high color temperature." In fact, it was like a "welder's arc," he said, only "whitish rather than blue." Around its perimeter were various "coruscations"— reflections and sparkles—that scintillated "in different colors with a strong tendency to red and pink." During his observation, he had a passing airliner and helicopter for comparison, and he also used binoculars. Through those looking glasses, the orb of light "seemed to be pinched in the middle, somewhat like an hourglass," as relayed by Hynek. All told, as it varied slightly in intensity, he got the impression that a radioactive source was in operation.

As it hovered for several minutes, it moved through small arcs in different directions, once darting southeast and upward, "as though directed," Hynek said. "It was variously described as jogging up and down, at random, and not quite at random but somewhat in a spiral, and generally as wandering," he reported.

Hynek reemphasized that "we are here dealing with the testimony of a man who is used to observing deviations of a few seconds of arc in guidance systems, and who is fully aware that there is a difference between illusory motion and real motion."

Three days later, Woodbury described a wholly different experience. While driving home from work on January 17, he spotted a "bright, ruddy, fairly large cloud standing by itself in the southern sky." He didn't dismiss it as a typical meteorological event due to its distinctive form and the fact that it appeared to have "uniform illumination clear to the edges."

His account is accompanied by a sketch of an object that is loosely teardrop-shaped with a long spiraling tail.

Per investigators, the first sighting was simply deemed "unidentified"; the second, vaguely as "other (cloud)."

Another pithy Project Blue Book report dated April 22 comes from Belchertown in the western part of the state. The witness reported something resembling a "torpedo with a small dome" with flicking blue, yellow, and red lights. It seemed to be hanging close to a B-52, according to the observer, and traveled on a straight course until it disappeared behind a mountain. The account is accompanied by a sketch of a large, perfect circle with a row of lights at its top; it bears striking resemblance to the Death Star, which would be immortalized a decade later in *Star Wars*.

The conclusion? There was "insufficient data for evaluation," according to investigators.

Meanwhile, on April 1 in New Braintree (a bucolic hamlet in the north-central region of the state), a boarding school student described viewing a red, glowing "plasma cloud." When a hysterical friend suddenly banged on her door, she looked out to see a fiery orb descending into the dark woods. As the pair watched, several white circular objects seemed to converge around the weird plasma cloud, rapidly covering "tremendous distances," flying "at very high speeds and unbelievable angles."

"They seemed to be able to go from about a half mile to three miles away in an instant!" she marveled, noting that they saw as many as 11 in the air at once.

While she and her friend never saw them again, there were numerous rumors about "strange things in the sky"—although it was very "hush-hush," she added, as "nobody wanted to be labeled a 'kook.'"

Two and a half months later, on July 15 in the nearby city of Springfield, another observer reported a UFO so "enormous in size" that it blotted out the sky from horizon to horizon. It was gray/silver in color with numerous tiny lights along its underside— red, amber, white, blue, and purple. Its bottom was flat, and its sides seemed to bevel up, "even though," the observer reiterated, "you could not see the ends of the craft because of its size." Most mesmerizingly, bolts of electric current bounced off it, "arching at will."

Meanwhile, earlier in July in Dennis on Cape Cod, a strange craft showed up an otherwise spectacular July 4 fireworks display. A group of onlookers oohing and aahing at the colorful starbursts, flares, and spirals suddenly spotted a saucer shape hovering above the treetops nearby. It was almost as if it were watching the fireworks, too, as one of the witnesses would later report to the Mutual UFO Network (MUFON). The large metallic disc resembled "two pie pans put together" and was rimmed with several blinking red lights. "It was extremely fast and made no sound at all," the witness reported.

Six large windows spanned its spinning lower half—three clear, three red-tinged. "When the clear windows spun around, you could see inside, but I didn't see any figures or shapes of things, only shadows."

The saucer hovered for several minutes and then turned and shot off in a straight line to the west.

The sighting was followed up with an even stranger event later that evening. The witness and a friend headed back to the lake, lying down on the dock to watch the night sky. All at once the water seemed to be pummeled by hundreds of large, dense objects (what they assumed were rocks). They came out of nowhere, splashing and kerplunking into the lake—yet not one hit the startled teenagers or landed on or even grazed the dock. Needless to say, "we got out of there pronto," the witness recalled. "I do not know if these two events are related, but it sure felt like they were."

Years later, he claimed, he randomly struck up a conversation with a complete stranger at a diner; remarkably, he had also summered on Cape Cod that same year and described the UFO down to the exact detail, clear and red-tinted windows and all. (It really is a small universe, isn't it?)

THE BRIDGEWATER TRIANGLE

Briefly, it hovered: an unmistakable triangle. Unlike anything he'd ever seen.

Then, with a burst, it shot off, blotting out the stars and the inky-black sky as it passed overhead and disappeared into the dark depths of the night.

"Up to that point, I had been 100 percent skeptic," Boston-area news reporter Steve Sbraccia recalled in the 2013 documentary *The Bridgewater Triangle*.

And while the experience with this UFO didn't immediately make him a card-carrying ufologist, it did crack open a door in his brain, allowing for the possibility of otherworldly phenomena.

You'd certainly never mistake it for Bermuda—but Massachusetts purportedly has its own mysterious "triangle." A swath of land in the southeastern portion of the state, the so-called Bridgewater Triangle is profuse with unexplained phenomena, including numerous UFO sightings.

Encompassing 200 hundred square miles, it stretches from Abington to Freetown to Rehoboth, thus embodying a rough triangle shape—although the area is considered by many to be elastic; its borders shift depending on the teller of the tale. The majority of stories, sightings, and odd experiences proliferate from two distinct areas: the Freetown–Fall River State Forest and the roughly 17,000-acre Hockomock Swamp, which spans Bridgewater, East Bridgewater, Easton, Norton, Raynham, and Taunton.

Within its depths, there have been supposed run-ins with Bigfoot and other inexplicable creatures (such as the ever-impish "pukwudgie"), as well as all manner of ethereal sights, sounds, ghosts, phantoms, and apparitions. Suggesting something anciently sinister, the swamp is home to a number of odd and unusual wonders, as well, such as archaeological and geological oddities and primitive etchings.

All of this has in turn proved a natural draw for the darker side of humanity: The triangle has been the site of satanic rituals, gruesome murders, grave robbing and desecration—and an unusual number of people have disappeared within its wilds.

Attracting ufologists, cryptozoologists, ghost hunters, and paranormal researchers from around the world, Massachusetts's triangle has been the subject of numerous books, theses, TV shows, and a full-length documentary by filmmakers Aaron Cadieux and Manny Famolare.

Sbraccia, for his part, experienced his encounter along State Route 106.

Driving unassumingly along the rural byway that runs east to west between Plainville and Kingston, he looked up to see something completely unusual: a giant, illuminated object, diamond-shaped—or, as the baseball fan described it, resembling a home plate—and spanning the width of five 747s flying tip to tip.

Meanwhile, headlines from local newspapers over the years blared, "Mysterious Balloon over Bridgewater!" "UFOs over Randolph? Some Persons Say Yes!"

In the 1970s particularly, sightings of strange craft were widespread. A few examples: In August 1973 a diamond-shaped object was seen hovering for several minutes above Scituate; in December 1975 a silent, spherical, rotating object with a shiny metallic surface and hieroglyphic-like etchings was spotted moving south over North Attleboro; in November 1976 a large orange-yellow sphere that seemed to pulsate with energy was witnessed imploding, disappearing, exploding, then rematerializing in the skies over Taunton.

These purported run-ins with the strange and unusual continue to this day. There have been reports in recent years of gigantic rotating discs; luminous ovals; fireballs; plummeting objects of bright neon green; a sextet of orange lights moving in formation in a straight line, then a circle, then back again; triangles with green lights moving back and forth and side to side at unfathomable speeds; and clusters of bright orbs seeming to move together and escorting one other.

IT SMELLED FROM OUTER SPACE

Encounters with unidentified objects can be terrifying, exhilarating, confounding, life-altering.

And apparently, in some cases, extremely potent.

In April and May 2013, the south-of-Boston city of Quincy experienced a spate of strange aircraft sightings that were accompanied by an overpowering assault on the nostrils.

"Unbearable." "Horrible." A "mix of sulfur and rotten eggs." Or, as one resident less delicately described it, "like poop."

The scent-bombing craft appeared in the sky over the city on several successive nights and weeks—although only when it was clear and cloudless—flying low, humming, circling, and looping for hours on end.

If all that weren't vexing enough, the official response only served to raise more questions.

Sources with the Federal Aviation Administration (FAA) told local media that the aircraft was not a drone, that it was in fact manned—but not per local or state directives. All FAA spokesman Jim Peters would say to WBZ radio was, "we have to be very careful this time" concerning information.

Meanwhile, the FBI responded to a query with the terse reminder that the agency "does not comment on aerial activity." (The always-enterprising Fox Mulder and Dana Scully of *The X-Files* might have some very different thoughts on that.)

"It's frustrating, it really is," City Councilor Brian Palmucci told reporters, noting that he repeatedly received the flat response, "We can't tell you that" when attempting to get answers from federal agencies. (Such as: Was it a law enforcement exercise? Could he at least tell people it was nothing to worry about?)

As for that stench? Living so close to the ocean and marshland, residents' noses get used to the full spectrum of salty, sweet, putrid, and sulfurous scents that result from the normal breakdown of organic matter.

This one was so odious, though, that the city hired chemists from Boston to test for bacteria. Those tests ultimately came back negative, and the city never could determine what it was or what in the world—or not of this world—caused it.

Still, it's not the only recorded case of a UFSO (an unidentified flying *smelly* object). Lowell to the north experienced something similarly bizarre and even more grotesque in 1846. What was characterized as a "luminous flying disc" spun into view and spewed a "fetid-smelling jelly" down upon the prosperous mill city. A large piece of the rancid mass was later collected, weighed, and measured—it was a dense 440 pounds and 4 feet in diameter.

Without a doubt: a bona fide close encounter of the gross kind.

PROJECT BLUE BOOK FILES

Over the 22-year history of the federal government's Project Blue Book program, some 12,000 cases were reported and probed. Of those, nearly 200 emanated from the Bay State. The cases included here were officially deemed "unidentified" or "unknown," while several weren't considered suitable to be labeled in even those vaguest of terms, with no conclusion reached at all.

On June 10, 1949, in the skies "southwest of Boston," a military pilot spotted a large white flying tube. It was about 100 feet long and traveling at least 150 miles an hour in a peculiar perpendicular fashion. It generated no sound, trail, or exhaust. The pilot, identified as a member of the 58th Fighter Squadron out of Otis Air Force Base, sighted the object about six miles away from his aircraft at an altitude of 30,000 feet. He reported chasing the object until losing track of it in the overcast.
Conclusion: "Insufficient data for evaluation."

On February 8, 1950, above Teaticket (a tiny town on the lower tricep of Cape Cod's flexed arm), a group of pilots sighted a pair of illuminated cylinders climbing high in the western sky "at great speed." The occurrence was unusual enough to be reported by the *Cape Cod Standard-Times*, which identified three of the men as Marvin Roger Odom, owner of the Falmouth Airport; Philip Foushee, a former navy fighter pilot and lieutenant; and Raymond Wood of Falmouth, a student pilot and employee of the Woods Hole Oceanographic Institution. As they "intently watched" the western sky from the Falmouth Airport around

5:10 p.m., these airmen "with thousands of hours of aerial background and experience" spotted two odd-looking objects emanating a "queer light," according to the newspaper. The unusual craft flew 25 degrees above the western horizon, converged, then drifted apart again. They were so bright at first that the men first spotted their reflections while inside the airport ready room before going outside to investigate.

"I've flown regular aircraft and jets, and I'm familiar with weather balloons and that sort of thing, but I've never seen anything like these objects," Foushee said. "They appeared to be cigar-shaped, and although they operated as a pair, they weren't attached in any way, as they differed in their distance apart."

Odom agreed, describing them as "far away and very bright," with "long cylindrical bodies that weren't attached but were apparently maneuvering."

Suddenly, as the group watched, something seemed to drop from one of them. Foushee described it as "a blaze dash, a sort of fireball with no smoke."

After a few minutes performing maneuvers, the objects climbed rapidly high into the sky and disappeared.

"They were entirely different from any type of aircraft I've ever seen or heard," Odom said. "They just don't resemble anything."

He added that "for years I've pooh-poohed this flying saucer stuff. Now I've seen something that's beginning to make me wonder." **Conclusion:** "Unidentified."

On September 30, 1950, in Provincetown, on the tip of Cape Cod, three researchers involved in a weather radar project tracked a bizarre unidentified object during their regular monitoring. It blipped onto the radar in the vicinity of an F-86 Sabrejet and was tracked for nine minutes. According to Project Blue Book investigators, considering the observers' "apparent qualifications," it was "deemed advisable" to interview them about the encounter.

That interview was conducted three days later by senior airman Thomas R. Yandoh. The officer identified the principal observer as having worked with radar since 1945 and serving as a research associate with the Massachusetts Institute of Technology (MIT) and as a staff weather officer with the 67th Fighter Wing of the Massachusetts Air National Guard. His colleagues included an analyst from Brockton and an electronics technician from Dorchester.

Their mission consisted of tracking two F-86 aircraft flying north from Provincetown to the Isle of Shoals in southern New Hampshire; the purpose was to establish wind velocity, which, they pointed out, was being done as a "personal favor" to someone named Tuttle. The "exceedingly puzzling event" occurred when the planes were on their third run, heading northwest at 30,000 feet. Another plane seemed to accompany them—except in due time, they could determine that it was no ordinary craft.

"It was moving very rapidly," according to the principal observer, and "caught up with, passed, and then crossed the course of the 86s." It then made a tight turn to the right, passing directly over—or under, they couldn't be sure—the path of the planes they were tracking. "Figuring conservatively," its speed was 1,200 miles an hour, while the centrifugal force exerted on it during its abrupt turn was something more in the 5-G force domain.

The pilots were alerted to its presence but didn't report anything, which, the observer noted, was "not too surprising" considering its speed and the fact that it may have passed several thousand feet above or below them. "It gave an excellent radar echo which could not be mistaken for anything else and in all respects except for the velocity seemed a normal radar target," the observer wrote in a follow-up letter. "Now I wish we had taken some accurate velocity measurements when we had the chance."

He mused that "the whole thing doesn't seem to make sense, as you will discover when you reflect a moment about it. It was very evidently an interception of some sort of our flight, but what? The turn was utterly fantastic; I don't think the human frame could absorb it, but if the object was radio controlled, it had no particular business flying on such courses on planes occupied in legitimate business."

He added that doing rough calculations on control surfaces and angles just makes things more puzzling and indicates that the object was "entirely unconventional in many and basic respects." What bothered him most, he added, was that it gave off a "very good radar echo," implying irregular surfaces and comparatively large size so that the pilots might have seen it. He suggested running another mission for the purpose of "luring it out again," tracking it, and getting pilots close enough for a look—although "they'd never catch it I'm sure."

"It seems highly probable that I may be poking into something that is none of my business, but on the other hand, it may be something that the Air Force would like to know about if it doesn't already," he concluded. "The whole thing has us going nuts here, and we don't know whether to talk about it or keep our mouths shut. Until I hear from you, we will do the latter."

In the 15-page report, the message is relayed between officials that the matter should be considered strictly confidential. **Conclusion:** "Unidentified."

On December 21, 1950, at Westover Air Reserve Base in Chicopee (in western Massachusetts), a witness spotted a half-moon-shaped object moving south along the horizon. It had rounded edges, a silvery outline, and maintained a "continuous whistle"-type sound, like "wind blowing over wires or objects of slight resistance, and maintaining some semblance to the sound of jet propulsion." There was no evidence of exhaust or lights, and the object remained in sight for about 45 seconds, flying between 10,000 and 20,000 feet in the air. "It is not believed that any observable celestial phenomena or planets could account for the sighting," the investigator stated. It was most likely metallic, its speed "appeared to far exceed that of known aircraft," and it "disappeared suddenly without apparent reason."

The investigator identified the observer as an employee of Remington Rand Company, a member of the Air National Guard at Westfield, and an aircraft mechanic with experience "as such in World War II."

"The observer stated that he was familiar with the sounds of all types of conventional and jet aircraft and that the sound which attracted his attention was different from these." He concluded of the interview that the observer "appeared sincere and requested no publicity," was nervous during his interrogation, and was "slightly reluctant" on details. "He stated [that] he wanted no one to think him carried away by the 'flying disc' theory."

Conclusion: None stated.

—⬩—

On April 17, 1952, in Longmeadow (also in western Massachusetts), two engineers observed an object that was "four times as bright as a star" moving erratically and making "rapid climbs and dives." Round and deep-orange-colored, it was in constant motion, traveling between 600 and 1,000 miles an hour, at times elongating and changing shape, as well as emitting a shaft of light from its underside. It was up at least 15,000 to 20,000 feet and emitted no exhaust and emanated no sound. The observer, identified as a 33-year-old

graduate of the Massachusetts Institute of Technology and employed at American Bosch Corporation in Springfield, described it as "larger than any known conventional aircraft" and stated that he had "never observed an object similar to this in the heavens."
Conclusion: "Unknown."

On April 24, 1952, in Milton (in southeastern Massachusetts), two civilian electronics engineers observed a pair of "flat, flexible, square-like objects" wobbling and undulating through the sky. The men were employees assigned to the radar systems laboratory in the electronics research division of the Cambridge Research Center; they spotted the objects through a high-powered scope while standing on top of the US Air Force observation platform at the summit of Great Blue Hill. Per their estimations, the craft were about 10 feet long, of "undetermined thickness," dark orange or red, with seemingly no aerodynamic features and producing no sound, trail, or exhaust. They moved about four to six miles across the sky in a matter of a minute and a half. The observers described their course at first as a "rapid ascent" from 1,500 to 2,000 feet, then an "unsteady horizontal plane," followed by another sudden rapid ascent. They moved at about 150 miles an hour, rising together at an angle and disappearing into the haze.

The radar systems at the tower were inoperative at the time of the incident, according to the investigator, but the main witness was adamant that the objects "were not kites, birds, large pieces of paper, or resembled in any detail aircraft known to him." Furthermore, his description was not "influenced by any material which he has read on the subject of unknown objects."
Conclusion: "Unknown."

On July 16, 1952, in an event that gained national attention, a US Coast Guard photographer observed and photographed four bright lights over the Salem Coast Guard Station north of Boston. Using his Busch Pressman camera, Shell R. Alpert, captured 16 photographs—2 8 × 10s and 14 4 × 5s. Alpert described the quartet of bright lights alternately brightening and dimming—almost, as it were, attempting at a signal. Their color temperature was a "high number of Kelvin degrees, extremely brilliant and white," he said. The photos were analyzed by the Air Force's photo reconnaissance lab, and photocopies are included in the report, depicting a V pattern of bright white orbs above—and seemingly headed toward—the Coast Guard building.

However, when analyzed by the Air Force's photo reconnaissance lab, they were deemed as "open to doubt because there are no reflections of the object on nearby parked cars." Nevertheless, the Coast Guard made the photos public on August 1 due to the "widespread public interest in aerial phenomena." They were picked up by *Scripps Howard* and the *New York Herald Tribune*, among other news outlets. Still, the Coast Guard mulled over the odd story for a decade, eventually reporting perplexedly that "it has never been determined what caused the phenomenal lights." **Conclusion:** "Unknown."

On July 23, 1952, in Nahant (north of Boston) coast guardsmen made a report of two "bluish lights" moving through the air. They were about five feet in diameter, flat, disc-shaped, moving without sound or exhaust trail at a speed faster than a four-engine airliner and at an altitude of 1,100 to 2,000 feet. The objects then made a sharp turn, gained altitude, and disappeared.

Conclusion: "Unknown."

On July 24, 1952, at the Massachusetts Correctional Institution at Norfolk (south of Boston), three prison guards observed a "slow-moving greenish object" traveling north to south at a low altitude. It was round and flat—pancake-shaped, according to one of the witnesses—about five feet in diameter, black, tilted at an angle, and "drifting along slowly" between 60 and 225 feet away from them. It was up at least 50 feet off the ground and disappeared behind one of the buildings of the colony. Although no aerodynamic features, trail, exhaust, propulsion system, or engine sounds were noted, the unusual object was followed by a loud rushing noise. As one of the witnesses stated, "the night was dark but the object seemed darker. It made no noise; to me the night seemed to get quieter as I watched the object."

Conclusion: None stated.

On October 10, 1952, at Otis Air Force Base on Cape Cod, three airmen described a "blinking white light [that] flew upward, then started a pendulum-like motion for 20 minutes." The object then disappeared "by shooting straight up at a terrific rate of speed."

Conclusion: "Unknown."

On February 26, 1954, in Newburyport (north of Boston), four witnesses reported a "disc type silver object" that was "extremely loud and intense." They were alerted by its jetlike roar and ran out to see something the size of a silver dollar with a dark center, a white ring, and a whitish trail or tail. One of them provided a sketch that depicts a round object with an amorphous, almost amoeba-like center labeled "dark" and a trailing line labeled "haze." It was overall silvery-white, "much brighter than the scattered clouds in the distance," and "unquestionably at a very high altitude."

The investigator named the observers as "reliable" and surmised that it was a "possible aircraft" sighting—although no known aircraft were reported to have been in the area.
Conclusion: "Unidentified."

On August 27, 1954, in Dorchester (south of Boston), a witness described as a military source reported a half-dozen teardrop-shaped objects moving in formation. They were each "as large as a bomber," alternating between white and blue, and left no exhaust or trail.
Conclusion: "Unidentified."

On July 30, 1959, in Assonet (in southeastern Massachusetts), an observer reported a moon-sized object coming out of the northeast and heading directly toward him. It made a steady humming noise and was initially yellow-white before morphing to a dull red. A 30-year-old male who claimed to have more than 500 hours of flying time (both dual and solo), the witness said he "began to be afraid of this alien object as it moved slowly but steadily toward me." He ran down a hill, tripped, and rolled, then hid beneath an overpass while, he claimed, the UFO stopped directly above him. When he looked at it, he said, he "felt a strange tingling" in his spine, and his nervous system and parts of his body "felt like pins and needles." Finally the light went out, and he "had the feeling" that the UFO had left.

Conclusion: "Insufficient data for evaluation."

—✦—

On March 25, 1960, in Dalton (in western Massachusetts), a husband and wife reported a very peculiar incident (even in Project Blue Book terms): A 30-pound chunk of ice hurtled out of the sky and landed on their property. The local newspaper published a photo of Mr. Larry Roche standing and pointing at the object. According to the Project Blue Book report, the area was surveyed by an investigator, and there was no overhead object visible that the object might have been dropped from or fallen out of. The ice's "spatter pattern" was a fairly even distribution over an area of 28 feet by 28 feet. The ice was analyzed and described as porous, or like rime ice. "It resembled tapioca snow and was considerably less dense than ordinary ice, for it was quite coarse, and a chunk the size of a man's head probably weighed not much more than a pound. By no consideration could the frozen snow-ice be thought the same as the surrounding snow and ice."

Conclusion: None given, although the report's investigator noted that "future cases may indicate a pattern which will lead to a conclusion."

—✦—

On October 6, 1961, in Sharon (south of Boston), participants in and spectators of a soccer game were halted by a strange sight in the foggy, misty sky. As described in the report, they were "five sharply outlined objects standing still at times and rushing away. Always in formation; moving west. Observed during daylight. Silver-white color." One of the witnesses, referred to as a 14-year-old male student, said the objects disappeared "in a fraction of a second; I couldn't even notice their disappearance, it was so fast." He added, "I don't think there is material yet known that it could be made of."

He finished his account by requesting more preprinted information forms so that "the next time I see a UFO, I will not have to type them up myself."

Conclusion: None given. However, the investigator noted vaguely that "the conditions were present for atmospheric refraction of light from an unknown source."

———

On November 1, 1962, in Woburn (northwest of Boston), a witness gave a highly detailed account of a bizarre object he viewed for nine minutes (as timed by his watch). In broad daylight, he spotted a craft that he estimated to be 40 feet long, 30 feet wide, and 15 feet high. It had a circular dome top, a flat bottom, and a black band—what he thought might be a "catwalk"—around its lower edge. Glowing a golden orange, it was brighter than the sun, "extremely small," and appeared at an altitude of 2,000 feet, he claimed. The observer also submitted a drawing and noted the presence of a rectangular periscope-like protrusion that extended and retracted from its underside and was accompanied by clicking sounds "as if taking pictures of the land below."

The craft remained relatively stationary and then simply vanished as he was watching. Immediately following the encounter, he claimed to feel suddenly overpowered with sickness. Three photocopied newspaper clippings are included with the report; they describe the witness as Charles Kirk, a carpenter. He told reporters that the strange object looked "like a streamlined egg cut through the middle." According to those reports, a civil defense official discovered a slightly abnormal amount of background radiation at the site.

Conclusion: The sighting was chocked up to "imagination" or "psychological" factors due to the fact that the witness didn't summon anyone else to corroborate what he was seeing. Also, there were no other reports of anything similar in the area.

On December 1, 1962, in Arlington (west of Boston), an observer spotted a red object "shaped like a frankfurter" that appeared to be "tumbling end over end in a straight flight" from an 85-degree elevation in the northwest to a 30-degree elevation in the southwest. It was about the size of a "one-sixteenth" screw when seen from a distance of 30,000 feet. The observer reported that he attempted to get a telescope but could not focus in time before the object disappeared behind a stand of trees.

Conclusion: The investigator concluded that it was "probably a high flying jet" because the sun was low in the west and the observation was toward the west. "The red color is attributed to the sun," he wrote.

On May 26, 1964, in Cambridge (just outside of Boston), respected researcher J. Allen Hynek provided testimony from a witness who spotted a "very thin ellipsoid" crossing the sky. According to Hynek, the observer was a pilot, worked as a satellite tracker in Iran, and was a "reliable fellow and not excitable." The object in question was a "pretty good oval" about 15 to 20 feet in diameter, "dead white," cocked to one side, and following a completely straight trajectory. It had "no bumps on it at all" and would most resemble "two pearly white picnic plates glued together," Hynek relayed. It also seemed to have a demarcation between its top and bottom.

Hynek went on to describe it as about one-third to one-half the size of the full moon and "exactly the color of a metallic surface reflecting cumulous clouds." He emphasized that it could not have been a plane because it passed behind a cumulous cloud and that the viewer had seen other aircraft in the area and identified them, including three twin-engine Fairchilds and a transport craft coming in toward Hanscom.

"We have another unidentified that falls in the general pattern of rapidly flying discs in straight trajectories," Hynek added. **Conclusion:** "Unidentified."

On July 29, 1964, in Franklin (west of Boston), an observer reported "objects resembling lights the size of trailer truck tires dancing in the trees from dusk till dawn." The lights blinked in a succession from red to blue to white, and there was one off by itself that was green and shaped like a boomerang. The witness claimed to see the lights several times over a period of months near their home, and they often interfered with the electricity. The investigator, however, pointed out that no report was made until a popular TV program featured a story about UFOs. "The observation could be attributed to ground lights, witness imagination; unreliable report," they wrote.

Conclusion: "Insufficient data for evaluation."

On September 4, 1964, in Brookfield (in south-central Massachusetts), three girls reported a trio of UFOs circling Lake Quaboag.

They watched from the Pine Lane side of the large water body, using binoculars to spot first one, then two, then three objects rotating over a period of two hours. They were each "completely red, oval-shaped" with protruding poles and Saturn-like rings around them. They flew at high speed, rotating several times, before disappearing faintly. The compiler of the report noted that the sighting was "characteristic of a misinterpretation of an 'astro body' such as a star/planet if the motion is confined to a small area of the sky." It could have possibly been aircraft, as well (or both), he wrote. **Conclusion:** "Insufficient data for evaluation."

On September 6, 1964, in Westfield (in the Pioneer Valley to the west), a group of at least 10 people claimed to see what they described as a "mother ship" and a quartet of smaller ships "performing" in the air for about eight hours. The report was submitted by well-known UFO researcher Raymond E. Fowler (who lived in Massachusetts). The consensus of the witnesses was that the mother ship arrived first, drifting in from the southwest close to the ground. The size of a "dollar bill held at arm's length," she had a red pulsating light at her bottom and red and white lights at each end that blinked alternately. Soon, four smaller ships "came out" of her; they were the size of a silver dollar held at arm's length, and each was equipped with a single pulsating light. One zipped off to the north and disappeared; a second hung over the mother ship and then headed south, where it hovered; the other two went to the southeast, hung there, then began slowly swinging, pendulum-like, from the east to the south and then back to the east. Eventually, all but one—the one that had vanished to the north—converged back on the mother ship, which resumed her drift along the horizon before disappearing. Some

witnesses also claimed to see several cargo planes and jets approach from Bedford, circle the larger ship, then fly away again.
Conclusion: "Unreliable report."

On October 28, 1964, in Brimfield (in south-central Massachusetts), several neighbors reported seeing an object that was "all lit up," shaped like "a derby hat," and the "size of a large car." What's more, it appeared to have several windows spaced two feet apart. It was initially seen as a flash of light, then it rotated up and down about 10 to 15 feet above the ground for about three hours. During this time, the witnesses claimed that their television sets and electricity noticeably dimmed. Local newspapers also reported on the incident, identifying an Irene Page who "had observed a sparking ball of light which intermittently scouted her property." As she told reporters, it "would seem to waver off, flying up and down like a bird," then return periodically.

The investigator, though, reported "no auroral activity in the area at the time," an absence of searchlights, and absolutely "no physical evidence of any object or person having been in the area of the alleged sighting." He commented that, "in my opinion, this was a publicity stunt. My reason for saying this is that Mrs. [BLACKED OUT] is a recently widowed mother of four children. There is ample evidence of poverty in her house. There is possibility that she fabricated this account for the purpose of attracting attention and sympathy for herself and her family."
Conclusion: "Unreliable report."

CONTEMPORARY CASE FILES

In December 2004, a couple in Billerica (northwest of Boston) reported a harrowing near-abduction experience to the Massachusetts Mutual UFO Network (MUFON). According to the group, husband and wife "Robert" and "Anne" were standing out on their deck when they claimed that a huge craft zoomed up and hovered above their house. All of a sudden, they were illuminated in a circle of blinding bright light. Shielding their eyes, they looked up; a separate blue beam then shot down, settling on Anne. To her husband's horror, she began to levitate above the deck. Robert said he then grabbed her by the waist, pushed her into the kitchen, followed closely behind, and slammed the door.

Moments later, he looked back—but the light and the craft were both gone.

MUFON investigators came out to search the neighborhood and home and to question the couple. They even placed an ad in a local newspaper, but no one came forward to corroborate the story. The couple remains baffled and frightened by the encounter.

In early 2009, an observer of a UFO claimed that his videotaped evidence was destroyed by real-life men in black (although he never saw them to know for sure). Driving in an unspecified area of western Massachusetts one night, he suddenly saw a circular, brightly lit craft zip by in the sky. It had at least a half-dozen lights that were either the traditional "color of light" or a dim red. "Time and dust [have] buried my memory on an absolute certainty of the color," the witness wrote in an online reporting forum. As the object hovered above a nearby house, he jumped out of his truck and took 30 seconds of video with his Samsung Gravity phone.

The next day he went to work as usual, leaving his phone in his truck because there is "ZERO cell reception" in the "big brutal architecture job" where he works. Later, at lunch, he went out to check his phone—and there it was, 10 feet away from his truck, "crushed to oblivion." The car was still locked and undisturbed, nothing else broken or removed, he claimed. He couldn't find a SIM card among the wreckage. "I know it sounds like a made-up story, but it's as true as I can recollect, and I'll never forget it," he wrote. "I still wonder what happened."

On March 3, 2011, in Lowell, Joe Souza was hanging out with friends near Floyd Street when he looked up and exclaimed, "What the heck is that?" Up above his neighborhood there was something big with strange glowing lights; as it hovered and hummed, it rapidly changed shape, transforming from a triangle to a square to a kite.

"It looked like something out of a movie to me," Souza told reporters. He shot video of the strange object, which received tens of thousands of views on YouTube and drew the attention of the popular Syfy Channel series *Fact or Faked*. After Souza posted his footage, other locals reported that they, too, had seen the mysterious object and wondered what it was and where it had come from. Souza, for his part, noted, "I have always thought something else is out there, and I always needed to see proof. This is my proof."

On July 31, 2011, in Acton (west of Boston), an unnamed motorist photographed a "reflective, black, tube-shaped object traveling in an easterly direction," according to MUFON. In a report accompanying his image—which was captured with a 35-millimeter camera—the driver described the object as 30 feet long and roughly 6 feet in diameter. He first spotted it when it was about 200 to 300 feet in the air and snagged his photographic "evidence" when it was between 1,000 feet and 1,500 feet away and still traveling east. In the photograph, the unidentified object appears as a fuzzy, elongated blur.

———

In December 2011, strange glowing lights were captured in photos and videos in the skies all along the south shore of Massachusetts, from New Bedford to Swansea. The ensuing photos were then posted all over social media. In those blurry images and shaky videos, a series of orange and reddish lights can be seen floating in formation and at times hovering soundlessly. "They were glowing like fireballs," witness and amateur videographer Abdulelah Elmalli told local reporters. "One of them changed colors from orange to a reddish color, a bloodshot red, and moved down very slowly" before quickly ascending. "I thought 'This is not natural. This is not something you usually see.'"

Local radio talk show host Ric Oliveira also reported something "disturbing" above Swansea: It appeared to be a large, angular tube that swiveled and glowed a deep red. Then suddenly, it curled into a ball and slowly lifted off.

Other locals reported seeing similar airborne lights throughout area parks, drifting silently before burning out—but many assumed them to be sky lanterns, an Asian tradition that involves wrapping rice paper around a small bamboo frame containing a candle (although in 2012, Chinese New Year wasn't until late January). The Federal Aviation Administration did not receive or investigate any reports of UFOs in the region, a spokeswoman told the local media.

Oliveira, though, was emphatic, taking to Facebook and YouTube with pictures and videos. "When something 300 feet long changes shape in front of your eyes, that is no lantern. This kind of shakes you to the core because your whole reality changes."

He added that, if it was some kind of military vehicle, "I'm glad we have it, because it will scare the [expletive] out of anybody."

———

In January 2013, officials backtracked on their response to numerous sightings of a strange object above Amherst and Pelham. On January 8, residents in both western Massachusetts towns described something dimly lit and either diamond-shaped or triangular moving slowly and silently above the ground (up some 75 to 100 feet or so).

Representatives from the FAA, Westover Air Reserve Base in Chicopee, and Bradley International Airport in Windsor Locks, Connecticut—which is responsible for radar reports in western Massachusetts—all told reporters at the time that there was no record of any aircraft traffic above Amherst or Pelham. A couple of weeks later, though, a public affairs chief with Westover confirmed that a US Air Force C5 cargo plane had taken off from the base around 5:30 p.m. on January 8 and returned around 9:30 p.m. Still, according to Lieutenant Colonel James Bishop, it would be hard to mistake a C5 for the quiet, low-flying triangle that was widely reported. "There's just no mistaking it," he told the *Daily Hampshire Gazette* of one of the world's most imposing aircraft. "It's quite a loud sound and quite a big aircraft."

———

On February 11, 2014, in Stow (a MetroWest suburb), a husband and wife were perplexed to see a giant wingless craft in the air outside their living room window. As they reported to MUFON, they ran out and looked up; the object was hanging about 200 to 300 feet in the air above them. It was queerly shaped, mostly square with a triangular front and rounded edges at its back end. They guessed it to be 30 feet long, with several large bright lights in alternating white, blue, green, and red. It was very quiet, only putting off a slight humming sound. The wife reported feeling a "strong energy," a kind of "current" or "buzzing" passing through her body when it was near, "like I was having some energy maybe directed toward me." She accompanied her testimony with a sketch. It depicts an amoeba-like shape with a sextet of dots at its center and a line of lights around its rim (labeled "From above me [the] underside of craft") and a second drawing looking a bit like a fuzzy caterpillar with six spots (labeled "Coming directly towards us").

On May 20, 2017, in Plymouth, a witness reported seeing a silent, black, triangle-shaped UFO moving low overhead, according to MUFON case No. 83881. The witness described it as slightly blurry-looking with one white light at each of its three points. "There isn't much more to tell," he stated. "I immediately knew I was seeing something not of this world."

In June 2017 in Chelmsford (northwest of Boston), a witness reported seeing two unusual objects in the sky above her wide-open front yard and driveway. As she told MUFON, the first object was in front of the second one (which was about 20 feet behind and slightly to left). They maintained this constant formation, flying steadily "almost as if there was a rod between them to keep them together and maintain status," according to the witness, who added that there was "absolutely" no sound. "I have never seen any object in the sky in my entire life that looked like this."

Eric Hartwig, the state director of MUFON, told the news site *Wicked Local Chelmsford* that he spoke with the woman, who said the objects were metallic, with a "lattice-like appearance, like under a porch." She also provided a crude drawing of what she claimed to have seen: two rectangular-shaped objects with a crisscross at their narrowest ends. Hartwig surmised that it could have been a small homemade experimental mechanism, which can give off the effect of ion propulsion. "That's just what I thought of when she described it," he said.

On January 2, 2018, in Northampton in western Massachusetts, a witness reported a "black wing" about 50 to 100 feet long hovering alongside Interstate 91. "At first I thought a new construction crane had been set up to the side of the highway because of two bright, stationary lights over the top of the trees," the witness stated in his testimony to MUFON in case No. 89280. As he approached, however, he realized that it was a giant craft; he could make out its silhouette because it was much darker than the sky. It hovered several hundred feet in the distance and was at least 500 feet high, with bright lights on its underside and several along the front edge of each wing. He added that he thought he could see windows and could "kind of make out an interior space." "It wasn't until I drove under it that I clearly saw the wing shape," he stated. "I tried to slow down as much as possible. . . . I then realized this was something I've never seen before, and it was just floating, silently."

On February 8, 2018, in Bolton (a MetroWest suburb), an observer reported a large black form hovering above Interstate 495. It was about 500 feet up, moving very slowly, and seemed at first to look like three or four lights moving in a tight line formation. The observer could make out no telltale flashing FAA lights, writing that, "I tried to think if maybe they were helicopters or military planes, but they were too low, slow, and tight together." Then he was able to see a red pulsing light—dimming and brightening—and the craft's full shape took form: It was a triangle with three white lights at each tip and a red light "smack in the middle." The lights were rounded, not sharp, and the underside of the craft had a faint metallic shine to it. The observer said it looked "exactly" like the triangular UFOs that were spotted in the skies throughout Belgium in the 1990s. "I have been an amateur UFO enthusiast for years and have learned to debunk about 99.9 percent of most sightings," the witness wrote. "I am a skeptical believer and have maybe seen two to three interesting things in the sky before. This was a legit sighting of a UFO by definition."

On March 11, 2018, in Swampscott (on the state's north shore), a witness reported seeing an oval object bedecked with three lights that moved "super-fast" above the bare tree branches. Its lights were lined up horizontally—two were a flickering bright white; the third was a pale orange. They were hazy, growing steadier as the craft slowed. It moved in a "smooth, forward, slightly descending southeast direction," before abruptly stopping and hovering at a height of 200 to 400 feet. The witness described jumping out of his car and watching as the object evaporated into thin air. "It literally became transparent in about one to two seconds," he stated, while at the same time suddenly darting sideways and disappearing. Several seconds later, the observer claimed to see a helicopter coming northeast from Boston, casting a bright searchlight. "The bizarre object I saw was not an airplane, blimp, or any other known craft," the witness wrote. "It was terrifying in its speed and disappearing or cloaking maneuver."

On March 12, 2018, in Gloucester (a north shore fishing village), a witness described a rotating, brightly lit, morphing craft. Appearing in the west-northwest sky at about 65 degrees above the horizon, it first looked like 10 stars, each the brightness of Sirius, arranged in a rough circle. It was predominately white and mostly remained stationary; when it did move, it zigzagged in "impossible turns." And then: The circle changed, the top flattened, and it looked like a traditional flying saucer. Just as rapidly, it changed back again.

In June 2018 in Chatham (on Cape Cod), following a power outage, several observers described seeing several beautiful and strange craft of various sizes dancing in the sky. The primary witness described going to check out the extent of the blackout; when he looked up, he saw a giant red light heading toward an area known as Forest Beach. It was not a blimp and was way too low to be any sort of plane. He and some neighbors drove down to the beach, and "as soon as we got there we look up in the sky and there are at least 15 to 22 beautiful flashing lights," he said. They were "darting around, zipping left to right, up and down, flashing on and off, putting on the most amazing show right before our eyes. It looked like a Christmas tree made out of low-hanging stars." Then he noticed the original red saucer, now much clearer—large, red, and definitely with a structure and girth to it. It hovered from right to left, occasionally blinking, with each blink doubling then tripling in size. When it came in contact with any of the other flashing lights, it melded with the light, seeming to absorb it, growing larger as it did. Eventually it slowly moved away and disappeared out over the ocean.

On June 10, 2018, in Yarmouth on Cape Cod, witnesses sitting on their deck noticed several very bright lights that seemed to be "wriggling." When they retrieved a telescope, the brightest light "wiggled like an insect." As they adjusted the lens of their telescope, they could see lesser lights moving along its perimeter and a central bright light that shone in a constant manner.

On September 8, 2018, in an area between Topsfield and Georgetown (north of Boston), a motorcyclist reported seeing an oblong object over Interstate 95 North. It had two large white lights closer together than a car's headlights and a row of lights along its length in a pattern of red, white, white, and red. Not once did it move. Riding beneath it, the witness could make out four dull orange-white lights in a square pattern, with a black horizontal line crossing its middle. And around the square? A jet-black manta ray shape. "It was bigger than a helicopter or Piper Cub plane," the witness said. "It was half the size of the biggest jet. It looked like it was just suspended in the sky."

And, indubitably, to be continued . . .

Two

VACATIONLAND

It's Out of This World

Looking at these stars suddenly dwarfed my own troubles and all the gravities of terrestrial life.

—H. G. WELLS

THE SKY WAS RED-ORANGE—IT SEEMED AS IF IT WAS ON FIRE.

The 27-year-old housewife huddled in the dark, watching, all at once perplexed, scared, and fascinated. Her adjusting eyes could make out a large round object amid the glow; in fact, it seemed to be the source of it. It was the size of a jet fighter, the color of gold, the brightness of the sun (only not so harsh on the eye).

"It was brighter than anything I know of," she would later insist, adding that "gold" was just an approximation of its color, as it was like "no colors I have ever seen."

Silently, it rotated, looking like a cup turned upside down on an elongated, oval platter.

Then, in a moment that churned her stomach, she spotted something she couldn't quite explain—not forms, exactly; not even an outline; but something hazy, giving the impression of many "things" making hurried movements in the open space between the craft's flat bottom and half-moon top.

"I just can't explain it on paper, but there was life there, I'm *certain*. Nothing human, *but alive*," she later told investigators. "I don't believe we have any material such as this object was made of. Not that I have seen anyway."

Her conclusion: a spaceship. Without a doubt. "I'm certain it wasn't anything we have on Earth."

Fearful and confused as the experience made her, she noted that it was "beautiful, just beautiful. There is really no word I can describe it in exactly."

The above, purportedly occurring in the far northern town of Caribou on December 21, 1955, is among the thousands of cases of unexplained phenomena investigated by the federal government in the mid-twentieth century.

And, like many others before and after, the housewife's encounter was concluded to be of "unknown" origin—a mystery never to be solved.

Vacationland. It greets the many visitors at the state line who escape to Maine for its beaches, quaint seaside towns, and seemingly countless islands and peninsulas; many thousands of acres of pristine, rugged wilderness; and rural, inland oases spotted with lakes and ponds.

But perhaps "otherworldly" should be included among the experiences in travel brochures and websites about "Vacationland" (an indelible slogan adopted by the state in the 1930s). Just like its vast and varied terrain, there have been all manner of encounters with the unknown in Maine: countless sightings from the southernmost coastal towns to the northernmost wilds along the Canadian border; scares at military bases that spawned many a conspiracy theory; and one of the most highly publicized (and thus analyzed, scrutinized, and criticized) abduction cases in history.

With the state being one of the earliest-populated areas in North America (long before it was known as such), Maine also boasts one of the earliest-reported UFO sightings. On July 22, 1808, Camden schoolteacher Cynthia Everett recorded "a very strange appearance" in her daily journal. At around 10:00 that night, the 24-year-old saw a light proceeding from the east that "I at first thought was a métier." Quickly, though, she soon perceived that it was anything but. "It seemed to dart at first as quickly as light, and appeared to be in the atmosphere," she wrote. But then, just as rapidly, it "lowered toward the ground and kept on at an equal distance, sometimes ascending and sometimes descending."

Such experiences with erratically moving, unexplainable objects would repeat time and time again in the decades and centuries that followed—and likely will unceasingly continue—creating an explicable aura of mystery in Maine's skies.

A DIFFERENT KIND OF EXPERIENCE IN THE ALLAGASH WILDERNESS

It was supposed to be a two-week expedition of hiking, canoeing, and rustic camping; a getaway from the hubbub of the city and busy schedules. Ultimately, that's exactly what it turned out to be—but not at all the kind of "getaway" the four young men were expecting (or so they claim).

In August 1976, twin brothers Jack and Jim Weiner and their friend Chuck Rak, all students at the Massachusetts College of Art and Design, set out with guide and US Navy veteran Charlie Foltz. They first climbed Mount Katahdin, then chartered a plane to Shin Pond, where they set out by canoe on the Allagash Wilderness Waterway.

Their first bizarre encounter came about several days in, as they set up for the night at a camping area known as Mud Brook. Looking across the water, they saw a blazingly bright star—much brighter than all other celestial bodies around it. According to Jim, it "displayed a strange quality of light." Assessing it with binoculars, he determined that it was not a star at all but an object a few miles away, hovering about 200 feet above the treetops.

Suddenly, it blinked out, and the men soon dismissed it as they went about their night.

What happened two nights later, though, was much harder to put out of mind.

The group canoed into Eagle Lake, setting up at a remote campsite known as Smith Brook. Wanting to do some night fishing, they built a huge bonfire to serve as a beacon and then hauled their canoe into the water and paddled out into the dark night.

But about a quarter-mile out, Chuck got the "spooky feeling" that he was being watched—highly unlikely with the four men being, as it were, in the middle of nowhere. He turned to see a large, pulsing sphere of colored light; as big as a house, easily 80 feet in diameter, it hovered 200 to 300 feet above the cove.

Chuck described it as a "very, very bright globe of light" and changing color "from white to red to green in a liquid kind of melding motion."

The men stared at it, confounded. Thinking that it might provide some kind of answer, Charlie (the guide) picked up his flashlight and started signaling SOS in Morse code.

In response, the fiery orb flew in at a terrifying speed. It stopped about 50 feet above the canoers and shot out a cone-shaped beam that swept the water like a searchlight. Frantically, the men began to paddle, using both their oars and their hands.

But they didn't get far: The bright beam fixed fast on the canoe; they were absorbed in a warm glow.

And then the canoe was sliding back onshore, its bottom scuffing along the sand. The men stared back at their illuminated intruder, which now hovered a few dozen feet from them. It bobbed subtly in the sky, as if contemplating them—then it shot across to the treetops on the other side of the lake; finally it zoomed up into the sky and disappeared.

Feeling exhausted and drained, the men turned to see that the large fire they had built had burnt down to mere embers. Charlie would later marvel at the sheer impossibility of this, as "some of the wood we put on there was about the diameter of my leg," he told reporters. A good 10 inches in diameter or more, he estimated.

But with nothing much to say—and not feeling in the mood to talk—the men went to bed.

The next day, Chuck said, they talked about it but not for long or in any great depth. When they encountered a ranger on duty, they struggled to explain what they had seen. He quickly dismissed the sighting as lights from the grand opening of a hardware store in the town of Millinocket: Two guys in the back of a pickup were operating a searchlight.

Chuck later scoffed, "there was no way this could have been any hardware store grand opening." Not to mention that Millinocket was a good 75 miles away.

The outdoorsmen wrapped up their trip—welcomingly devoid of any more bizarre events—and returned to school and work. They never discussed "that night" at any length.

But soon Jack began having nightmares; in them he saw four-fingered, insect-like beings with long necks, large heads, and metallic glowing eyes with no lids. In one of his more vivid night terrors, he was being examined by them as Jim, Chuck, and Charlie sat on a nearby bench, unable to intervene.

He and his brother started reading up on UFOs and strange phenomena, and Jim eventually attended a conference hosted by noted ufologist Raymond Fowler. He approached Fowler, recounting the story; intrigued and excited, Fowler convinced the four to undergo regressive hypnosis.

And that's when their ordeal came out in vivid, disturbing details.

Under hypnosis, according to transcripts, each of the men described being trapped inside a tube. It was dark and swirling with sparkling, dustlike particles; at the end of it, they were somewhere with numerous machines, silver examination tables, seemingly endless hallways, and chambers.

Jim caught sight of the creatures, which were thin, spidery, and clad in bodysuits. "They're like bugs! They've got, ah, bug eyes," he exclaimed. Chuck, on the other hand, found he had difficulty focusing on the aliens—whenever he tried, it was like "trying to tune in a fuzzy radio station."

Pencil sketches the twin brothers drew later would depict beings with elliptical eyes, beaky mouths, turkey-wattle necks, willowy arms, and thumbless hands.

All the men recounted being naked and in a zombie-like, almost paralyzed state. They obeyed telepathic commands. They submitted to intrusive, sometimes painful pokes and prods of their eyes, fingers, legs, toes, and genitals. They didn't speak; they didn't move.

Toward the end of the agonizing experience, Chuck recalled reentering the portal, the sensation of downward movement.

Then they were back in the boat. None of them paddled; the canoe seemed pushed by an ethereal force. When finally back onshore, they watched the fireball disappear—it was over.

There was no way to know how long they were aboard the craft. Later they would say it was maybe two hours.

Fowler found their descriptions to be mostly consistent. They all passed lie-detector tests, and all were deemed mentally stable. The men were also able to make detailed sketches of the entities, the craft, and the examining instruments.

All of this would eventually be outlined in Fowler's book *The Allagash Abductions: Undeniable Evidence of Alien Intervention*, published in 1993. The men would soon gain international fame—and ridicule. They appeared on an episode of *Unsolved Mysteries* and *The Joan Rivers Show*. All except for Charlie would report other alien encounters; Chuck would later recant his affirmations about the abduction part of the story, although he would affirm undeniably, "Oh, yes, I saw the craft."

The other "witnesses" remain steadfast in their stories, despite the wide range of response that continues to this day.

"This was the 1970s, so the reaction from others was to ask what we were smoking, drinking, or dropping," Jack told the *Bangor Daily News* years later. "It's hard for people to understand, but I don't blame them. If someone told me a story like that, I'd say show me a picture, give me some physical evidence."

He added that was exactly what he hoped would occur—evidence to prove the "'Allagash guys' weren't crazy after all."

Because, ultimately, "we don't even understand what the hell went on there that night."

LORING—THE NOTORIOUS MILITARY ENCOUNTER

For two nights in October 1975, a strange hovering craft caused chaos across Loring Air Force Base, tripping off radar, sending personnel scattering—and ultimately spawning theories and conspiracies about UFOs and military and government cover-ups.

The events unfolded on October 27 at the Aroostook County base—one of the largest in the United States at the time but decommissioned in 1994—in a dramatic, *X-Files*–like fashion.

Around 8:00 p.m., an air policeman patrolling the nuclear weapons dumping area spotted an unidentified aircraft approaching the north perimeter of the base. It was flying low, no more than 300 feet aboveground, and it had a red navigational light and a white strobe light.

Around the same time, the radar lit up; tower personnel reported an unknown craft about 10 to 13 miles east-northeast. They attempted contact: no response.

Immediately, the entire base was put on alert; any unannounced, unknown aircraft was considered a threat. A ground sweep ensued.

For an estimated 40 minutes, the aircraft moved around the base, seemingly exploring, taking particular interest in the heavily guarded weapons storage area (coming within an estimated 300 yards of it). Yet pursuing personnel were never able to get a fix on the object, which zipped along fast and moved in ways that were "helicopter-like," according to news reports at the time.

Then it zoomed off toward New Brunswick, disappearing from sight and dropping from radar.

Eventually, activity at the base resumed to normal—relatively, at least. The local media was inquiring, high-ranking officials were calling and visiting, and many an unanswered question plagued the minds of base personnel.

And then, it happened again.

The following night, airmen reported a silent, orange-and-red object hovering above the runway. They described it as solid, looking like an elongated football, and about four car lengths long. It seemed to have no doors or windows, and no propellers or engines were visible.

This time, an Army National Guard helicopter out of Bangor was deployed to help track it down; several years later, Chief Warrant Officer Bernard Poulin would tell UFO investigators Larry Fawcett and Barry Greenwood that stories from the base and radio tower were erratic and contradictory. They never could spot any kind of intruding craft, he recalled.

Captain Michael Wallace, a pilot, also later related a confounding experience.

He was on duty the night of the second visitation, part of a refueling squadron assigned to Loring. Upon arriving on base, he recalled how he and other flight crew members—between 200 and 250 in all, he estimated—were summoned to a briefing. There, they were told about the previous night's incident. Wing staff referred to the craft specifically as a UFO, Wallace remembered, and described how it could hover silently, move unpredictably, and make "almost instantaneous" jumps from place to place. Support in the way of fighters and ground forces was being summoned. They were ordered to talk to no one.

Later, Wallace was on a routine mission south of New York in a formation of three tankers. The radio suddenly crackled with orders from the command post: The captain of the lead plane was ordered to transfer command to Wallace. He was then to depart the formation, retain radio silence, and fly with his lights out. His mission: to head directly to the base and get as close as possible to observe another unidentified craft.

Wallace said he watched as his fellow pilot "descended into the darkness" in the moonlit night. Now in command, he led the two tankers on their normal approach. As they arrived closer to base, there were many harried reports on the tower's frequency and the command post's frequency: "How did it get down there that fast?" "It's gone!"

The tankers landed as scheduled. In the normal postflight debriefing, Wallace noticed that the lead pilot was decidedly absent. A day or two later, he said, he ran into him and asked, "What in the hell happened with the UFO the other night?"

The answer was terse. "I can't talk about it." Then: "And you wouldn't believe me if I could."

That was the ensuing message and atmosphere across the base: Keep your mouth shut.

The son of an anonymous noncommissioned officer on duty both nights even claimed that his father's log and reports had been removed. Stationed in the area of the weapon assembly building during the first incident, he described to his son how he suddenly received reports from all posts, roving patrols, and even the gate staff about some kind of strange object flying around. He climbed to the top of a bunker and stood there, witnessing something "blindingly bright." But, he claims, his calls to the tower were met with dismissive replies.

As per routine, he went back to fill out his log and start a report. A few days later, Air Force personnel questioned everyone who had seen the incident firsthand. They then inspected his father's duty station and, he claimed, pulled out any reference to either night, replacing those pages with new ones.

After that, the matter was closed "for all intents and purposes"—and although he was never expressly told so by superiors, he knew not to speak a word about anything he had seen.

In sparse discussion of the subject, the Air Force would say it was a Canadian helicopter or a "black helicopter"—most often associated with conspiracy theories about government takeovers.

Ultimately, though, the military and the government went silent, offering no real explanation to the public.

The startling fact remains that, despite flying low around a US military base for an extended period of time, an unknown craft evaded capture. In fact, it couldn't even be kept in sight long enough for anyone to provide more than a cursory description.

Could it have been the Soviets? An unannounced test—like a pop quiz, if you will—of base security? Or something truly unexplainable and out of this world?

It's been nearly 50 years—but those questions remain.

COSMIC ENERGY

Ever hear of orgonomy?

No?

That's not a surprise. Unless you're a student of fringe scientific methods or a resident or visitor of the Rangeley area (where orgonomy's "discoverer" Wilhelm Reich resettled after World War II), it probably just sounds like a subject you dazed through in science class.

It gets a little "out there," but the gist is that orgone is a biological or cosmic energy—even a life force—that Reich claimed could be detected, measured, and manipulated. The Austrian doctor and scientist, a one-time student and mentee of Sigmund Freud, said he had detected "orgone energy" or "orgone radiation" under several circumstances, including in the sky at night through an "orgonoscope," a special kind of telescope he invented. It was omnipresent, he argued: in the ground, in the atmosphere, in space. It also had a color: blue or blue-gray.

Reich, who also controversially attempted to cure neuroses through the release of sexual energy, moved to Rangeley in 1942 to further his study of orgonomy. So devoted was he to the "science" that he named his home, laboratory, and research center

Orgonon. Now a museum, the angular stone structure—which appears both modern and medieval at the same time—is built high on a hill overlooking the area's many lakes and filled with an array of peculiar-looking devices.

Among these are insulated "accumulators" that were intended to absorb the cosmic energy and concentrate it. Subjects were to sit inside, naked, with the intended result being an infusion of renewed energy. Reich also constructed something he called a "cloud buster"—it looks a bit like an alien death ray from an old sci-fi movie—which supposedly removes orgone from the atmosphere, thereby shifting the atmospheric balance.

Despite his persistence and tireless research, Reich failed to convince many mainstream scientists of orgonomy's validity. He also gained the unwelcome attention of the Food and Drug Administration following a 1947 story about him in the *New Republic*. The governing body particularly took umbrage with his claims regarding his accumulators. They accused him of fraud, but the eccentric Austrian paid little attention until 1957, when he was arrested after one of his students crossed state lines with an accumulator. The strange, ultimately sad case of Wilhelm Reich ended at a federal penitentiary, where, shortly after incarceration, he died of heart failure at the age of 60.

However, while he was still studying orgonomy up in Rangeley, he was apparently also on the lookout for UFOs. A Project Blue Book report from January 28, 1954, identifies a male witness from the remote central Maine town who spotted two pea-sized objects "like bright stars." Only they were moving along the valley below his observatory and changing in both their brightness and color (from a bright yellow-white to orange).

Filling out an eight-page "US Air Force Technical Information Sheet," he describes the objects as a mile or more away, occasionally humming, and "about twice as large as Jupiter, when largest." He also includes a sketch depicting his observatory overlooking Spotted Mountain and Round Pond and indicating the location of the North Star and tall spruce trees. The unidentified object is drawn as a rough circle, arrows representing movement down and over the valley—like a "J" sitting on its back.

"Both objects moved as described in sketch, one at a time," he wrote. "The first had disappeared in [the] valley to the east, when the second appeared where the first had been, before it traveled among the trees, a few minutes previously."

Although his name (as was routine practice) is blacked out throughout the 19-page report, Reich's identity is unmistakable. In a box asking for "Other special training," he typed and wrote in, "Discovery of primordial cosmic energy (orgone energy) (life energy)." He also identified himself as a medical faculty member at a college in Vienna, Austria, in 1922.

He added that he observes the sky "as a matter of routine; this belongs to research in the realm of atmospheric orgone energy phenomena," including movement and glimmering of stars and different types of clouds. He also reports "similar phenomena" that were called to his attention in preceding months, including on several occasions in January 1954.

The official conclusion? The object was of "unidentified" origins.

Reich, undoubtedly, lived a life plagued by unknowns.

PROJECT BLUE BOOK FILES

Between 1947 and 1969, the government investigated roughly 80 cases of UFO sightings across Maine as part of its Project Blue Book initiative.

These are the several that remain unsolved.

In March 1945 in Belfast (midcoast), a hunter observed an elongated object, tilted downward toward the earth, flying very slowly. Then suddenly it crashed into some trees at the end of a clearing. The enormous craft, though, seemed undamaged—although dazed—as it rested briefly on the ground. It then lifted again with a humming sound, began to spin, released a shower of fine silvery threads, and rose straight up, disappearing in seconds.
Conclusion: None given.

On August 2, 1952, in Houlton (Aroostook County), a witness reported several disc-shaped objects flying in formation over the town. They were sighted while he sat on a wharf in the town park. Flying about 2,500 feet up at an estimated 1,000 miles an hour, they were transparent, "very light green," and moved in and out of formation. The witness, described as a 27-year-old male educated at the University of Maine and employed as a sales representative at US Rubber Company, told investigators that he had "no conceivable idea" what it could have been.
Conclusion: "Insufficient data for evaluation."

On January 1, 1953, in Oldtown (in the Penobscot area), an observer sighted a "round, small object, whirling on top, [that] looked like a star with a ring around it." It flashed on and off as it moved in a north-northeast direction, at times suddenly changing direction and color simultaneously. It would "spin, stop, spin in the opposite direction and spin again." The witness said it stopped once to flash the following colors in sequence: green, white, red, blue, and white.
Conclusion: "Insufficient data for evaluation."

———

On October 29, 1953, in Mapleton (Aroostook County), two round objects were seen emitting a "dark green glow" that morphed to white with a green-blue fringe. They were observed through 8X binoculars as they traveled on a straight north course. They made occasional triangular deviations and were soon trailed by a third object with a bright blue flaming trail. None emitted any sound. **Conclusion: "Unidentified."**

———

On April 24, 1954, in Hartland and April 23, 1954, in Pittsfield (both in Somerset County), two witnesses gave matching descriptions of an oblong, saucer-shaped object moving across the sky. It had a domed top with a brilliant flashing light. Silver-colored and the size of a silver dollar, the witness in Hartland described it as making no sound, sitting still, and leaving no exhaust trail. The Pittsfield observer, meanwhile, described both vertical and horizontal movement that created a "whirlwind and cooling effect." It also made a noise like the buzzing of bees. Both witnesses agreed that, as it disappeared, it rose vertically straight up and out of sight. **Conclusion (in both cases): "Unidentified."**

———

In July 1955, at least two reports came in about a round object flying around the area. The first was from Charleston on July 5; one round orange object appeared to the observer to go back and forth and then ascend "some" while moving in a straight line. It appeared to be far off and traveling very fast. Six days later, on July 11, a woman in Greenville reported a round and flat object with a light blinking on top. It was about the size of a four-engine aircraft, she estimated, but had no wings or tail. She claimed that it circled her four times, was silver and pink, and emitted a "flash" out of its rear assembly.

Conclusion: "Insufficient data for evaluation." "Possibly aircraft."

On December 21, 1956, in remote Mexico (Oxford County), a housewife reported that, over a period of nearly two weeks, a "bright glaring green object" had descended several times on her property. It was saucer-shaped—shaped like the cover of her Easy Spin Washing Machine, in fact, she said—three feet in diameter, and luminous. It was "the most beautiful shade of green that I have ever seen," she reported.

In its most intimate encounter, it came down at an angle over the swings that sat in her backyard about 75 feet from the house. It got about three feet from the ground, and "I thought for sure that it was going to land," she said. Instead, it immediately disappeared. Later, while outside, she noticed that there was a four-inch-long, "perfectly even," cream-colored slash on one of the bars of the swing. "We believe it touched the swing when it went over it."

She emphasized that her family lives about two miles from town; there are open spaces on both sides of the house and no street lights. Furthermore, she added, "I am not seeing things nor am I daydreaming. I am a busy mother with three children and a six-room house to take care of. I have no time to be making up stories or daydreaming."

The sighting was submitted to US Senator Margaret Chase Smith, who in turn forwarded the report to the secretary of the Air Force. Investigators said that "some indications of ball lightning are present" but questioned the witness's reliability.

Conclusion: "Hallucinations."

———

From September 3, 1957, this short and succinct report describes a sighting from Presque Isle Air Force Base: "Round object, size of silver dollar, white. Disappeared in clouds. Appeared to be zig-zagging." Investigators speculated that observers could have seen "a light attached to a radiosonde balloon launched to report upper winds under fog conditions." Or it could have been an aircraft, they concluded.

Conclusion: "Insufficient data for evaluation."

———

On December 28, 1957, in Livermore Falls in southwestern Maine, witnesses reported a small, round, red-and-white object that was "very bright and moving very fast." It moved from straight up to straight down, then proceeded along a straight line before disappearing in the clouds.

Conclusion: "Probably aircraft."

———

For the summer of 1958, well-known ufologist Raymond E. Fowler filed a report from witnesses in North Turner. They reported seeing a silver-gray object floating in a wooded area below tree level in the Androscoggin County town. It had revolving dome lights that pulsated and were "brighter than a welders torch." The lights were blue, and the craft itself had a "dull finish." It was in view for more than five minutes; at least part of that time, the observers used field glasses and reportedly took pictures (which were not submitted with the report). The object then disappeared "with terrific speed." Fowler, who didn't submit the report until 1965, claimed that the sighting was reported at the time to Civil Defense.

Conclusion: "Too old for investigation."

On November 11, 1959, in Portland, right around noontime, an observer sighted a "perfectly round object" that moved from a 75-degree elevation in the south to a 45-degree elevation in the north. It was solid, white, not glowing. "A grapefruit might resemble it if it were white in color," according to the witness. Its flight path was straight, and its speed was "excessive" and constant— although on at least one occasion it stopped and stood still.

"It was flying high and at a tremendous rate of speed, faster than any jet could possibly fly," stated the witness, described as male, 41, and employed as an elementary school principal. "It was not an optical illusion."

Conclusion: "Insufficient data for evaluation."

On January 29, 1963, in Loring, a sighting was reported by military personnel. In view for three minutes, it was described as a small white object crossing Sagittarius. According to the investigator, a further report was expected to be submitted upon landing and crew debrief; however, that report was never forwarded.

Conclusion: "Insufficient data for evaluation."

On August 20, 1963, and September 4, 1963, two similar cases were investigated in Auburn and Oxford Counties. From the former, neighbors reported discovering strips of tinfoil on their respective farms. These appeared immediately after a "large explosion" that seemed to come from the upper atmosphere. The source seemed to be a silver object with a trail that "burst into a ball of orange-colored flame." It shook buildings and caused smoke, according to the farmers. The investigator surmised that it was chaff from radar-jamming countermeasures.

Two weeks later, another farmer from Oxford County reported a strange hole in his backyard. It was 6 inches in diameter and went down about 13 feet. He assumed it to be the impact of an object falling from high in the atmosphere. A US Army demolition team was sent to help recover any objects that might be at the bottom of the hole or in the vicinity. They concluded that the chasm had been drilled by an auger, as indicated by marks on rocks nearby. However, there was "apparently no attempt at a hoax," according to the investigator.

The report is accompanied by six 8 × 10 photos, including photos of men digging, the excavation site, the marked-up rock, and the interior of the hole at different angles.

On February 16, 1966, in Brunswick (north of Portland), a motorist reported two objects in the same vicinity in the sky, seemingly interacting with each other. The first was described as being pancake-shaped and about 25 feet in diameter, with red, blue, and green lights at its edges that flashed "erratically." The object itself had no basic color, according to the witness. It had a big white floodlight in the middle of its "belly," and it appeared to be about 150 feet up and spinning at about 18 RPM. It made no discernible sound, hovered "for periods," then made "quick starts and stops."

About 35 to 40 minutes later, a second object came into sight. It was much larger than the first and also round, grayish-metal colored and generating a "smooth power sound." It came close to the first object and circled it three times.

Both objects then landed, the witness claimed—the first about three miles from his car, the second about a mile and a half from his car. He watched and followed the objects to the landing points and reported that, upon settling, the lights on the first object grew smaller and became salmon-colored. At around 11:30 p.m., both craft disappeared completely.

Conclusion: "1. Astronomical (Jupiter). / 2. Insufficient data for evaluation."

———

Between April 17 and 19, 1966, in New Castle (midcoast), several observers claimed to watch numerous objects moving around in the sky on several occasions—purportedly up to 15 at a time. "The objects turn, spin, and revolve in a circular direction," according to the report. Arranged in patterns and evenly spaced, they could be seen "darting freely" at times, then slowing, then racing. They also appeared and disappeared on a whim. Sightings occurred from different angles and at different times of day. Some were said to emit red flashes—resulting in even more of the objects materializing.

Three witnesses were identified in the report: a schoolteacher, a housewife, and a bank teller.

One described a particularly striking pattern of five objects: Four were disc-shaped and slightly larger than planets in the night sky; the fifth was cigar-shaped and about the size of a jet, leaving behind a "slight yellow" vapor trail. The disc objects rotated on their axis and followed a circular track when they moved, glowed silver, and emitted red, white, and blue. They moved from an angle 10 degrees above the horizon to one 80 degrees above the horizon.

"They turned, spinned, and revolved in a circular direction in a circular path," according to the witness. "There just is nothing which could look like it. I have no reason to believe it was anything but a UFO."

Conclusion: "Probably astro? Cannot confirm."

On May 13, 1967, in Webster (Penobscot County), an amateur astronomer sighted something oval, flat, and about "the width of a quarter icon" moving across the face of the moon. It was a yellow-white color, with two fairly bright lights—one on the forward nose, the other near the center. Also, to either side and at the tail end were parallel lines of light that moved right along with the object.

"It moved primarily like a falling leaf . . . sometimes making dashes at terrific speeds in a general flight path (northwest) that brought it over the ocean," he wrote. "I noted no fluctuations in the intensity of the light source."

He was in the process of photographing the moon in different phases and captured one image of the purported object; it is included in the report but as a photocopy that does not transfer any discernible image.

Conclusion: "Insufficient data for evaluation."

POST PROJECT BLUE BOOK

In 1966, a particular string of sightings spread across northern New England, including in Vermont; New Hampshire; and, on March 24, Bangor. According to the *Barre Montpelier Times Argus*, resident John King was so alarmed by a bright, 60-foot-long object moving low in the sky that he pulled his pistol and fired four shots. The craft immediately zoomed up and out of sight.

"I could hear the elderberry bushes scraping as the thing came toward me," he recalled.

Local police were called, and they described King as "visibly distraught" as he recounted what happened. The incident was not reported to the government, so there is no Project Blue Book file—although there were investigations of similar events around that time period in Vermont and New Hampshire.

Over several months in 1968, sightings were similarly reported along the Passagassawakeag River in Waldo County. Saucer-shaped UFOs were said to make multiple appearances, attracted, some surmised, to the high tension power lines running through the area. Witnesses claimed to see the craft hovering over the lines and then spinning off; some said they left a trail of sparks to indicate they were "powering up." Ufologists have commonly theorized that would-be aliens are attracted to the Earth's power sources, including nuclear plants and high-power electrical wires.

OTHER STRANGE CASES

On September 1, 1971, in Orono (Penobscot County), a student driving back to the University of Maine campus saw a red object floating stationary in the sky. Beneath it, a series of green and white lights were visible. On "impulse," he jumped out of his Volkswagen and ran down to where the object was, he reported years later. He claimed to see "several small beings in white suits with head coverings" who appeared to be busy taking samples of something. He ran back to his car, he said; when he looked back, the craft was in the same place but had changed from "red to light red to dull yellow to white" and had shrunk into a "small dot just like the TV picture tubes of the '60s used to do." What was now a pinpoint then shot into space.

He said he alerted police and posted fliers at the student union asking anyone else who had seen the object to contact him (he got no response). "This sighting really changed my life," he concluded.

On January 18, 1974, in Madison (Somerset County), two seventh-graders playing out in the snow saw a peculiar craft overhead that they described as large, oval, and "glowing chartreuse." It rotated, and the lights along its side blinked red and yellow. One of the witnesses later estimated its size at 1,500 feet in diameter, with a wider oval-shaped wing surrounding it. It was flying about 1,000 to 2,000 feet high, appeared in the west and flew directly east, and emitted no noise. When it disappeared from view, the pair claimed that it was immediately followed by three Huey helicopters.

———

On April 25, 1974, near Brooksville (Hancock County), two youths were going smelt fishing. When they reached the edge of the local pond, they noticed flashing colored lights off in the distance. After about a minute, one of them decided to blink his flashlight at it. That was apparently enough of an invitation—the lights moved silently in their direction, hovering just above the water. Writing about it years later on a UFO reporting website, one of the witnesses described it as saucer-shaped, with a dome bubble, and about 70 to 100 feet wide. The lights swirled yellow, red, and white beneath the craft. He added that he thought he could see silhouettes or shadows in the dome. Being decidedly "freaked out," he yelled to his friend, and they turned and ran. But his head was moving faster than his feet, it seems, because he tripped. When he stood back up, he called out to his friend. There was no response. Only silence.

This went on for a while, and he grew increasingly frantic.

Finally his friend answered, and they regrouped in the dark. They suddenly realized that all the fishermen who had been on the pond were gone. "Somehow a period of time is unaccounted for," he claimed, describing himself as a 59-year-old ex-marine "not given to hallucinations or visions."

"This experience has stayed with me my entire life."

⸺⸻

On June 15, 1978, in Orrington (Penobscot County), the *Bangor Daily News* featured this blaring headline: "Object in Sky Upsets Orrington Woman." The resident, who asked to remain anonymous, reported a "huge red ball of light radiating a lot of heat" that passed over her car as she drove along State Route 15 near Wheeler's Hill on the Brewer line. She felt "electrified," her car headlights went out, and "her car radio went crazy." After running her car off the road in a panic, she knocked on the door of a nearby house (but got no answer) and was able to flag down a passing pickup truck. According to the newspaper, she reported the incident to the state police, the FAA's radar tower at Bangor, the Bangor Police Department, and an Orrington constable. No one else in the area, however, had reported anything, and the FAA had logged nothing on its radar.

⸺⸻

On September 21, 1979, near Cape Elizabeth, a local police officer reported a "pulsating light" with an unknown shape that appeared to be moving north by northwest over the ocean. It was approximately 1:00 a.m. Another officer from a different town called to confirm the sighting, saying it was about five miles out over the ocean and "heading our way," the witness reported. Two Cape Elizabeth officers were dispatched to the shoreline, where they were able to see the object. One of them, a sergeant, estimated that it was about 500 feet above the ocean. When it was directly off the coastline, it made a sudden turn south and disappeared. A week prior, the poster recalled, a local lighthouse caretaker had called the police station to report a large object floating in the water about 100 yards off the rocks. When he ran to the top of the beacon to get a better look, however, it took off from the water, straight up in the air.

In November 1981 in Starks (Somerset County), Kenos Henry was working at a friend's farmhouse near Brann Mills Road when he spotted a low, hovering red light. He described being "filled with terror," when suddenly a red beam was directed at him. It got low and close, he recalled, then zoomed off to the left—and then instantly zoomed back to the right. He was able to see that it was a "solid object with a light attached to it." Frightened, he jumped in his car and pulled out onto State Route 43—and saw that the UFO was behind and following him. As he picked up speed, it moved faster, staying with him, getting closer and closer to the ground. At one point, it shot out a multicolored light beam toward him.

He stopped at a friend's house, banging on the door to be let in. Not surprisingly, they didn't believe him, so they all piled in the car with him to see for themselves. Soon enough, they did, and argued that the object was just the North Star or Venus—until it started to move, first down and then toward them. Henry recalled that it seemed to be almost passive-aggressive, backing off as soon as it got terrifyingly close.

Around the same time, local deputy Bud Hendsbee and his wife were driving along the same route in the other direction. They saw the kids stopped in the road, listened eye-rollingly to their claims about UFOs, and then continued on. But a couple hours later, on their way back from dinner in Farmington, they had an encounter of their own: A brilliant white light hovering close to the tree line dipped and began moving toward them. Hendsbee, shielding his eyes from the glaring glow, began backing away in an attempt to get away from it. The light settled to the right of his vehicle. The deputy rolled down his window and was surprised at the lack of sound.

"It's going to and fro, up and down, floating in the air," he told author Nomar Slevik in *UFOs over Maine: Close Encounters from the Pine Tree State*. "You don't know if the thing's going to come through your windshield like a bolt of lightning."

It didn't, though. He and his wife continued on their way. The light was no longer in pursuit—but they had their own fantastic story to tell.

—◦—

On March 18, 1984, in Alton (Penobscot County), a witness described a "mother ship sighting." It was headed due west on a crisp, clear spring morning and was so large that it at first seemed to be a huge cluster of stars. "This ship was extremely large and the most incredible sight I've seen in my life," the witness recounted later. "Such a massive ship . . . no sound, it seemed to float over us." It was at an altitude of 700 to 800 feet and moved along at a steady pace of about 25 miles an hour—not once deviating in speed. Most remarkably, the observer recalled, it had "no set shape." Instead, there were "hundreds of different shapes all over the entire mass" that were covered in white lights. "The lights would softly glow and then recede into the various shapes at different intervals," he said.

—◦—

On October 15, 1988, in the Orono/Bangor area, a University of Maine student noticed a light hovering over a sports field. It "sat still as if it were on a stand," he recalled, and about several hundred feet in the air. The witness described it as "about the size of a small school bus, but wider." It was flat and "shaped like a shortened home plate"—although more like a delta than a rectangle. The night was still and quiet, and it sounded a bit like "a jet engine with the volume turned way down."

In 1989 in Blue Hill (Hancock County), two amateur pilots flying a Beechcraft V35 toward Boothbay Harbor sighted an unknown craft as they banked left. Bill Reiff, a lawyer from Somesville, and Randy Rhodes, who worked for the Ellsworth Police Department, recalled that the strange craft instantly appeared at their plane's altitude and simply hovered.

"It wasn't shaped like any plane I've seen," Reiff told author Nomar Slevik, "and it was not generating light but seemed to be reflecting light."

It moved to their left, he recalled, changing color from a metallic, aluminum silver to a pinkish hue; hovered a while longer about 20 miles away; then shot off at a high rate of speed. The whole time, it had a threatening aura to it, Reiff said. "In my 300 hours of flying time, I can definitely say it was bigger than anything I've ever seen in the air," he said.

When he reported the object to air traffic control in Bangor, they quickly reported back that only two aircraft had been captured on radar at the time: his own craft and one other small plane.

On November 17, 1990, in Hallowell (Kennebec County), an observer was looking out his window long before sunrise: The stars were still "crystal clear." Then, within 30 seconds, the sky was "as bright as dawn." He could see across tree line and rooftops. Then he saw a ball about 600 feet overhead, moving toward Augusta. It flew "steady and straight" at a constant speed—and then suddenly made a 90-degree turn and bolted off toward Whitefield. Thirty seconds later? The sky had darkened back to the way it was, and the stars were visible again. The witness claimed that his uncle, who lived nearby, experienced the same phenomenon.

On June 30, 1992, in Millinocket (Penobscot County), a driver with several passengers in his Ford 4×4 pickup had a prolonged experience with a series of unknown objects. After he witnessed a bright flash and pulled over to the side of the road, his truck inexplicably died—no lights, no radio, no horn. He fiddled with the instruments and the key for about two minutes—and then the vehicle's dome light and headlights "slowly and eerily came back on as if someone was turning a rheostat," he recalled. The radio flashed 00:00.

This happened once more, to the growing dismay of his friends (they thought he was playing a prank). Then, to their right about 50 feet into the woods, the group spotted three red lights alternating in a triangle pattern. The lights moved slowly, gliding through the trees about 10 or 15 feet off the ground, parallel to the road. At the urging of his passengers, the driver put the truck in gear and kept pace with them, increasing in intervals from 10 to about 50 miles an hour. The whole time they had their windows down; besides the truck, there was no sound. Also, they noted, the lights seemed not to be impeded at all by the thick forest. They floated and blinked silently along in an uninterrupted line.

Soon enough, the lights won the race, pulling ahead. The last the witnesses saw of them, they were about 100 yards away and directly in the middle of the road.

Then they took off—poof—gone. "I stopped the truck and we all scanned the forest, sky, and behind us for any sign of them," the driver wrote. "Nothing. Just eerie blackness pierced by my vehicle's headlights."

He added that he took his truck to the garage the next day; the only thing mechanics found was that the positive post of the battery had a dark discoloration as if it had been overheated. "Either way," he concluded, "it was not a natural experience."

On July 26, 1992, in East Corinth (Penobscot County), a witness described a similar kind of "cat and mouse" game perpetuated by a large, brightly lit craft. They first spotted the object a couple hundred yards away in the field behind their house. As they watched, it came closer, approaching to about 100 feet. The witness was able to approximate it at about 100 feet long; cigar-shaped; its dark underside punctuated by deep red, green, and bluish-white lights. It may also have had windows. As it moved, it made a low-pitched humming sound; this turned into a high mechanical whining when it made any sharp maneuvers.

Panicked, the witness jumped in the car and drove off. The object followed. The witness then stopped, got out, and climbed up on the roof of his car. The craft approached "close enough that I could have hit it with a rock" and hovered.

Then it moved away south. The driver followed the craft at about 60 miles an hour before losing track of it. Then, as he pulled into the parking lot of a closed store, the object appeared again, moving in a big arc across the sky. Deciding to head home, the witness once more spotted the object trailing in the rearview mirror; again, it flew out of sight. It appeared one last time when the witness pulled back into his driveway. All told, the ordeal lasted about 45 minutes, according to the witness, who stressed that "this is absolutely a true story and the strangest thing that I have ever experienced!"

On August 15, 1997, in Denmark (Oxford County), a hiker viewed a red, elongated object that appeared to be banking in the sky. It seemed to have black portholes, and it glowed in the areas where its body met its wings. It was very thin and very silent. The witness reported that his sister had a similar encounter a few months later in the nearby town of Limerick.

CROP CIRCLES? IN MAINE?

In August 2002, witnesses reported strange lights and sounds that appeared to result in crop circles. On August 4, one witness woke up around midnight to strange "metallic-type noises." She could not determine where they came from. Meanwhile, another neighbor was startled awake around the same time by their dog, which was barking ferociously.

Then, around 2:00 a.m., another witness saw a bright flash of light; it was followed by a small, flashlight-sized ball of light that hovered over a hayfield across the street. She watched it bob around for a while; then it "went straight up in a beam of light" and disappeared.

Around noon that same day, the 16-year-old son of the owner of the hayfield discovered curious crop formations. His mother and stepfather notified the local police. Everyone seemed to agree that the formations didn't appear man-made. The hayfield owner contacted the National UFO Reporting Center, which in turn put them in touch with Cambridge, Massachusetts–based paranormal investigators BLT Research.

The next day, a BLT field team was on the scene, examining the circles and performing interviews. As researchers described, the hayfield is about two acres, rolls slightly uphill, and is at the end of a dead-end street. Taking up much of its area were three contiguous, flattened ellipses. The largest was 65 feet at its widest point; the middle, 35 feet at its widest; the smallest, 25 feet at its widest. Their edges were just touching, creating what researchers of this type of phenomenon call a "thought-bubble" design.

The plants were "fairly gently laid over," with thicker-stalked growth such as milkweed bent at the base. Very few plants appeared to be broken (a strong indicator that a mechanical, man-made object was used). All plants were swirled clockwise. "The initial impression of the crop lay was of fluidity, with a clear undulating character to the flow of downed plants," the researchers reported.

They recorded no compass deviations, cell phone failures, or camera malfunctions in the general area of the circles (as can often happen in these cases). They also performed a stopwatch check—one stopwatch left outside the formation, the other taken inside—which revealed no time differences. The team did, however, capture several pictures of light phenomena and anomalies (also typical to such incidents).

The consensus: The event was "genuine," based on the overall crop lay, the elliptical shaping, the off-center quality, and the fact that there was generally no breakage at the base of any plants. Added to that is the eye-witness reports, the disturbance with the dog, and the "remoteness of the location and our character-assessment of the people in the near vicinity," they concluded.

MYSTIFYING—EVEN FOR A SKEPTIC

Sometimes, no matter your proclivities or skepticisms, things happen that simply defy explanation.

This point was driven home for Brad Luker one night when he was, well, driving home.

In early November 2006, the 40-year-old power plant operator was driving along through Industry, a small inland mid-Maine town. Suddenly he was perplexed by strange lights in the sky. They were bright and hovering low. The avowed skeptic realized they were emanating from something above his car. He pulled over, got out, and heard what he described as a "quiet jet engine." Mystified and a little nervous, he looked around for the lights—and then something stopped directly above him, lingering for a few seconds.

"That's when it really freaked me out," he told the *Lewiston Sun-Journal*. A former naval intelligence crypto-technologist and avid camper, he knows the many blips, spots, streaks, and lights the sky can yield. But this was "really bizarre"—not way up high in the air but "way, way down here."

He later talked to the police but said he felt "kinda foolish" because, if it was some sort of secret military mission, they certainly wouldn't confirm it—and local police would have no insight into such operations.

Ultimately, he said he assumed it was a helicopter or a military plane. Still, he mused, "I don't know why they would fly it that low, and I don't know why they would be out in Industry, Maine. It really doesn't make sense."

THIS ONE TIME, ON FRIDAY THE 13TH . . .

On January 13, 2017, four friends driving late at night in the Orrington area saw an object flying silent and low over a local lake. At first they didn't think much of it. It was probably just a plane coming in—that area is close to Bangor International Airport.

But, as one of the witnesses relayed later to the Mutual UFO Network (MUFON), the object suddenly dipped 20 to 30 degrees and swooped in uncomfortably close. It went from being far off the road and fairly high in the air (about 500 to 700 feet up) to about 200 feet away from the car and roughly 400 feet above the road.

It was then that they could see that it was a black equilateral triangle, about 40 to 60 feet across, with glowing, bright red lights at each end; it also had a central glowing, white light.

"The way the object moved was very odd, and I was euphoric but terrified at the same time," reported the witness, who also submitted a sketch to MUFON of a silver triangle with purple lights at each corner. "The best way to describe it is the way a feather or a leaf falls to the ground and swoops side to side. After it swooped down close to the car, everyone started to have this moment of awe, yet [were] panicky."

The driver recalled pulling over, turning off the radio, and rolling the windows down as the object hovered. It was "dead silent," they said, "that too-quiet type of quiets."

Spooked, they decided to continue back home. Then, as they turned a curve, they saw a second object, "this bigger, triangular thing," on the Holden/Bucksport side of the lake. It seemed be heading directly toward the first object. They turned back—but then, in just the short distance it took them to return to where they had been, "Of course the object was gone, along with whatever the larger object was," said the driver.

Friday the 13th, it seems, isn't just for Jason Voorhees.

ADDITIONAL CASE FILES

Think the golden era of flying saucers has passed? Certainly not (at least not in Maine). Odd and eerie encounters continue to be posted and shared on witness reporting websites and across social media—and newspapers are eager to report the ever-quirky run-in with a UFO. Here are some close encounters from this millennium.

In mid-February 2007, the sky over Franklin County was apparently lit up with numerous strange lights of no obvious origin. According to the *Lewiston Sun-Journal*, calls flooded the sheriff's department from all over the rural mid-Maine county on the Quebec border: New Vineyard, Wilton, Phillips, Industry, and around Mount Abram. The lights were described as bizarre and low to the ground. "They were seeing, basically, a string of seven or eight lights low in the sky that were fixed," sheriff's department dispatcher Bill Hoyt told the *Sun-Journal*. "There [were] also reports of jet engine noises low to the ground."

One person who called identified himself as a jet airplane mechanic, Hoyt said, and described these lights in the area as "not like any he had ever seen." Others who called in said they looked like stars. The sheriff's department called a Federal Aviation Administration office in Boston that monitors air traffic in the area; dispatchers were told that the only air traffic recorded included a couple of routine air flights at 40,000 feet. "It was kind of odd," Hoyt noted. "All these reports were from different locations at the same time."

In December 2009, witnesses driving along State Route 46 from Bangor to Bucksport suddenly came upon what appeared to be a large, charcoal-colored object hovering at tree level. As it was "very close" and moving "very, very slow," they were able to get a good look at its underside, which was smooth and covered with illuminated panels. They reported to the Mutual UFO Network (MUFON) that it seemed to be covered with mud and was dripping water, with strings of kelp hanging off it. It could have been what ufologists call a USO—that is, an "unidentified submerged object," or something that is or has been in the water. The witnesses added that it had a white light at its underbelly that slowly morphed to orange. This light wasn't a single dot or beam but "more like a luminous panel." The craft didn't make a sound, was "not aerodynamic by any means," and did not seem to bother the trees it was floating over.

—⁃ ⁃—

On January 8, 2010, in Biddeford (York County), a driver and a passenger came over a hill to see a disc-shaped object. It was equipped with bright, flashing white lights and a red center light, the driver reported. "It seemed to just sit there and move away very slowly," he wrote. That was, until he started to pursue it, driving up to 45 miles an hour. "As we got closer it started moving faster and faster." Within a minute, it was out of sight.

—⁃ ⁃—

On May 17, 2014, 20 miles southwest of Houlton (Aroostook County), an 11-year-old boy burst into his father's room, terrified. He said he'd seen a large blue, spherical-shaped object that emitted an orange glow. It moved directly over the house then streaked away to the south. At that point, the child said, a bright blue flash lit up the sky "like it was the middle of the day." This was reported by four other people in Houlton, as well as in New Brunswick, Canada, the previous night.

—⁃ ⁃—

On September 9, 2014, in Augusta, a family of five driving along Interstate 95 spotted a triangular object against the "bluish-pink" sky. As they reported to MUFON, it was about 100 feet up in the air and made a perfect triangle, and at each vertex of the triangle there was a white light. These lights appeared to be equidistant from one another. All family members agreed that it was a flat metal color, with no shine to it and that it featured what looked to be subtle seams. It was silent; it hovered and never moved. "This object was so out of place that it was difficult for us not to notice it," reported the 44-year-old father, a mathematics teacher with a PhD.

———

On June 13, 2015, in Orrington, a driver going north on State Route 15 spotted a "bright teal" object slightly above the trees. It was moving north-northeast, dipping at times, with lateral motion back and forth. It seemed both triangular and circular, with smaller circles underneath it, the witness reported to MUFON. It was an unmistakable teal, and its bright glow seemed to emanate from within. It tipped slightly, then dipped below the trees and out of sight. The viewer reported that he thought he might find people outside using drones (but saw none). Also, there was no differentiation in the lights' color scheme to indicate the conventional aircraft bow/stern or port/starboard night-flying configuration. He also included a penciled sketch of the object: What it looked like "tipped away"—something like a more bulbous three-leaf clover—and "in profile"—similar to an upside-down saucer.

"This object was clearly not a conventional aircraft," he wrote, noting its ability to move "very quickly" back and forth and up and down. "The color was almost as bizarre as the behavior itself."

———

On August 20, 2015, in York, a driver spotted a high, bright light that at first "looked like a planet" and then became blindingly bright. Pulling over, the witness watched as the pinpoint of light swooped down in a path like a "J," coming closer and getting larger and brighter. It was disc-like, dark, and "absolutely silent"; and while it was helicopter-sized, it didn't appear to have wings or rotors. There were lights in three separate areas: Along one entire side was a red "panel" of glowing light; along the other, another panel of greenish-blue light. It was "VERY scary," the witness wrote, adding that they are not the "UFO type." "I can't explain what I saw, I know what an airplane or helicopter looks and sounds like; this was silent. WOW!"

On April 2, 2018, in West Paris, an observer watching a deer feed in his field watched as a "small dark sphere" floated by. Its diameter was no more than 16 inches, and it was only about 3 feet off the ground. It passed quickly through the yard, sliding along with a "brilliant, somewhat flat, bright reddish-orange glow." As it passed, only about 30 feet away, the area took on a decided chill. He added that he's seen such glowing objects more than once in the woods behind his house.

On August 12, 2018, in Albion, a stargazer hoping to get a view of the Perseids from his back deck was instead transfixed by three solid lights that were "brighter than most stars." They appeared slightly southwest and were moving in an easterly direction at about 90 degrees above the horizon. They moved about the speed of a typical plane or drone but maintained a steady, unbroken chevron pattern. This was accompanied by a low rumbling sound, "similar to a plane but an octave or two lower," the witness reported. A few seconds later, another bright light caught the viewer's attention. It was at first stationary; luminous; due east; and, like the chevron formation, about 90 degrees above the horizon. But then it began to move toward the chevron pattern, its luminosity reducing as its speed increased. Then, as the lone light approached the chevron, both objects became fainter, "eventually disappearing in the middle of the southeastern sky."

THREE

NEW HAMPSHIRE

The Roswell of the East?

Any sufficiently advanced technology is indistinguishable from magic.

—ARTHUR C. CLARKE

IT APPEARED AT FIRST AS A MERE TWINKLE—SIMILAR TO ANY OF the bright celestial dots that spatter the sky on a clear night. But as the Bowe family, driving along in the Nashua area, got a better look at it, they quickly realized that it was much larger, brighter—and closer—than any star.

It moved slowly above the trees, hundreds of feet off the ground. An unmistakable boomerang shape. Streamlined and aerodynamic. Making no sound. At its underside was a distinct pattern of lights: three larger and bright white; two smaller and amber.

The Bowe family was confounded. And fascinated. In fact, upon returning home, dad Jim quickly set to making calculations and drawings and even worked with his son and another graphic artist to develop sketches and 3-D renderings.

Many others across the southern half of New Hampshire would report similar sightings in the ensuing days and nights, ultimately drawing the attention of the national media; UFO researchers; and believers, skeptics, and agnostics alike.

"I've never seen a craft that could do that—being that big—float by without falling out of the sky and not making a sound," Bowe commented to reporters. "The wings were about the size of two tour busses. That's how big it was."

Occurring in early October 2014, the sightings of this "boomerang" were among the most prolific and detailed of contemporary times. Most notably, they served as an indication that UFO activity—as well as an overall interest in the abundant mysteries of the skies—hadn't waned in the Granite State.

New Hampshire has come to be known as somewhat of a magnet or "hot spot" for UFOs; the fifth-smallest state has even earned the moniker "Roswell of the East."

This can be attributed to the large number and varying range of sightings across the latter half of the twentieth century up to the present day—but most significantly, to two seminal UFO encounters that purportedly occurred here.

The infamous Betty and Barney Hill "abduction" in Lincoln in 1961 was the first-ever widely publicized account of an alien abduction. It was also the first real characterization of aliens as nefarious, probing beings, and according to researchers, it would establish the relative format of abduction accounts going forward.

The so-called Exeter Incident of 1965 was similarly publicized nationally and internationally, spawning support and ridicule, prompting a lengthy investigation by the federal government, and inspiring an annual festival that draws people from all over to the midsized southern New Hampshire town.

Both the Hill abductions and the incident at Exeter remain unsolved, and they continue to be analyzed, discussed, and referenced to this day.

So what is it, exactly, about New Hampshire—or, at least, its skies?

Some point to the nuclear presence in the state, including the long-running power plant in the southern coastal town of Seabrook, as well as the Portsmouth Naval Shipyard on the New Hampshire–Maine border, where nuclear subs undergo repairs.

Others note a much more ancient presence: The southern inland town of Salem is the site of "America's Stonehenge," a complex of man-made formations dating back 4,000 years. Composed of chambers, walls, and ceremonial meeting places—and believed to be the oldest human-assembled structure in the United States—it serves as an accurate astronomical calendar that can still be used to determine specific solar and lunar events.

Whatever the cause—which we'll likely never know—let's explore the state's long, intertwining relationship with the unknown.

EXETER EVENTS: "I SEE IT! I SEE IT!"

Just before 2:30 a.m., the door to the Exeter Police Department slammed open.

In rushed 18-year-old Norman Muscarello, shaking, stammering, attempting to put words to "the thing" he just saw.

Exeter being a relatively unassuming town, it was an unexpected and startling intrusion for the officers stationed inside: Patrolmen Reginald "Scratch" Toland and Eugene Bertrand. But they attempted to calm the boy's nerves as he began to tell his story.

This is what he claimed happened in the early hours of September 3, 1965: He was hitchhiking home from Amesbury,

Massachusetts, and, after his last drop-off, walking along State Route 150 past one of the many fields that lined the dark and rural roads of Kensington (about a half-hour from the Exeter line).

Suddenly he was shocked by bright red lights coming at him. Attached to an airborne object "as big as or bigger than a house," they zoomed in from seemingly nowhere and then hovered silently above him. The crimson lights pulsed around the rim of "the thing" as it slightly bobbed in the sky. Then, slowly, it drifted over to the roof of a nearby house. Frightened, the teenager dove into a ditch on the shoulder of the road. He then gathered himself, ran to the house, and banged on the door in an attempt to alert whomever was inside. But there was no answer—or any indication that anyone was home.

Muscarello then ran back to the road, flagged down the next passing car, and hitched a ride to the police station. All told, the whole thing lasted about 15 minutes, he said.

Quite the amazing story. Bertrand, though, surprised the boy by telling him it sounded like something he'd heard earlier in the night. While out on patrol, he came across a car parked at the State Route 101 bypass; inside was a crying, terrified woman who claimed to have been followed by a "huge, silent airborne object" with flashing red lights.

Eyes widening at the similarities, Muscarello insisted that one of the policemen accompany him back to the spot where he'd had his encounter. Maybe that would provide an answer. Or maybe the strange craft would still be there. Bertrand, although he surmised that it had been a helicopter, agreed, and the two headed off in a black-and-white back to the field along State Route 150.

They pulled over and got out. Bertrand clicked on his flashlight. The night was dark and crisp, silent.

The two started walking into the field, and Muscarello pointed behind him, his mouth dropping open.

"I see it! I see it!"

Bertrand turned. The area was suddenly glowing with light, and something—something very large—was cresting above two pine trees.

"My God," the officer said. "I see the damn thing myself!"

It was round, brilliantly lit, about 100 yards away. As they watched, it darted back and forth across the horizon, sharply turning, accelerating, decelerating. Muscarello would later describe it as acting "at times like a floating leaf." Its row of lights flashed in a rapid pattern, moving in succession from right to left and left to right: "1, 2, 3, 4, 5, 5, 4, 3, 2, 1," with each cycle lasting about two seconds. They were so bright that it was difficult to distinguish the object's true form.

At one point, Bertrand recalled, the lights came in so close that he fell to the ground and reached for his gun. Throughout the encounter, he estimated, the lights maintained an altitude of about 100 feet and a 60-degree angle to the horizon.

The officer radioed back to the station. A few minutes later, Patrolman David Hunt arrived; he watched with his colleague and the teenager as the lights moved farther off along the field then out of sight toward Hampton and the ocean beyond.

Back at the station, the officers called Hampton police and then alerted Pease Air Force Base in nearby Portsmouth. Soon the Air Force sent Major David Griffin and Lieutenant Alan Brandt to interview the three witnesses. The National Investigations Committee on Aerial Phenomena (NICAP) did an official inquiry, as well, with New England investigator Raymond Fowler compiling an 18-page report.

Fowler would later relate that "both the officers are intelligent, capable, and seem to know what they're talking about."

All of this piqued the interest of journalist John G. Fuller, who would go on to write several articles about the event and eventually publish the bestselling book *Incident at Exeter*. (In fact, his research at Exeter led him to learn about the Barney and Betty Hill abduction—occurring four years earlier in Lincoln to the north—which culminated in another book, *The Interrupted Journey*.)

With all the attention, the Exeter police station was inundated with calls from the media; pranksters; and other, seemingly credible witnesses. Toland—to whom Muscarello initially told his story—recalled one woman calling in "early, just before dawn," to report seeing something big, bright, and orange like a harvest moon. "All the time she was talking to me, her kids were at the window watching it," he told Fuller. "Now why would people go to all this trouble—people all over the area—if they weren't seeing something real?"

The official stance, however, wasn't quite so open to interpretation. After interviewing the police officers and Muscarello, Griffin, the Air Force investigator, sent a report to Project Blue Book staff, saying that "at this time I have been unable to arrive at a probable cause of this sighting. The three observers seem to be stable, reliable persons, especially the two patrolmen."

The Air Force soon released a statement claiming that the three men had seen "nothing more than stars and planets twinkling," ultimately attributing the event to "temperature inversion" and "multiple high-altitude objects."

Project Blue Book, meanwhile, came to the conclusion that the sightings were the result of "Operation Big Blast," a Strategic Air Command (SAC) training mission occurring in the area and led by the North American Aerospace Defense Command (NORAD).

Project Blue Book's supervisor, Major Hector Quintanilla, US Air Force, wrote to officers Bertrand and Hunt that there were also five B-47 aircraft flying in the area at the time of the sighting. Since no personnel engaged in the operation reported seeing unidentified objects, "we might then assume that the objects [you] observed between midnight and two a.m. might be associated with this military air operation."

The Exeter police officers took umbrage at this hit to their credibility. Bertrand and Hunt sent a letter to Quintanilla, dated December 2, 1965, at his post at Wright Patterson Air Force Base in Dayton, Ohio.

"We have been the subject of considerable ridicule," they wrote. "Since our job depends on accuracy and an ability to tell the difference between fact and fiction, we were naturally disturbed by the Pentagon report . . . and very reluctant to be considered irresponsible in our official report to the police station."

The weather was clear, there was no wind, so it couldn't have been "weather inversion," they argued. It was "definitely not" a helicopter, balloon, or military or civilian aircraft. They did see a B-47 in the area at the time, but it had "no relation" to the incident they witnessed. Furthermore, they added, Bertrand was a veteran of the Air Force, where he had been engaged in refueling operations with "all kinds of military aircraft." They also refuted Quintanilla's Big Blast theory, stating that not only had their observation been at 3:00 a.m.—an hour after that operation ended—but also official reports actually said the exercise had occurred a day earlier, on September 2.

"It was impossible to mistake what we saw for any [type] of military operation, regardless of altitude," they said. "We saw this object at close range, checked it out with each other, confirmed and reconfirmed the fact that this was not any kind of conventional aircraft, that it was at an altitude of no more than a couple hundred feet."

More than three weeks later, on December 28, perturbed that their initial letter hadn't received any kind of response, the officers again wrote to Quintanilla for "some kind of answer."

"We are still upset about what happened after the Pentagon released its news saying that we had just seen stars or planets, or high-altitude air exercises."

They reiterated what they had seen: a craft hovering no more than 100 feet in the air that "stopped, hovered, and turned on a dime" and that was "absolutely silent," "with no rush of air from jets or chopper blades whatsoever." In fact, the object had no wings or a tail. Meanwhile, it "lit up the entire field, and two nearby houses turned completely red."

"What bothers us most is that many people are thinking that we were either lying or not intelligent enough to tell the difference between what we saw and something ordinary," they lamented. "We both feel that it's very important for our jobs and our reputations to get some kind of letter from you to say that the story which the Pentagon put out was not true; it could not possibly be, because we were the people who saw this, not the Pentagon."

Muscarello also ridiculed the Air Force explanation, holding fast to his account and his experience. He soon departed to the Midwest to prepare for training as a naval officer. According to his younger brother Thomas, he was followed there by a camera- and microphone-toting press corps. With the Navy threatening to kick him out over the hubbub, the naïve 18-year-old signed numerous waivers to get rid of his unwanted entourage. As his brother told the local news site *Seacoast Online*, he didn't understand the legal jargon and fine print—allowing his story to be told, retold, and told again without any profits coming to him or his financially struggling family.

"They took advantage of him," Thomas said, further emphasizing his brother's credibility by adding, "He didn't receive a penny."

His family was similarly hounded by calls and visits from reporters, researchers, neighbors, and other curious locals. Then there were the camera crews that camped out on the lawn.

He also recalled the "stern" officer from Pease who came knocking to interrogate his mother, adding that officials seemed "very, very upset with what happened."

Norman Muscarello went on to serve three tours of duty in Vietnam. He died in December 2010 at age 55. Even though he was an "exceptional brother, son, and veteran," he was dogged until the day he died—he was perpetually "the UFO kid," the "Close Encounters guy."

Officers Bertrand and Hunt, for their part, did receive a shade of vindication: In January 1966, Lieutenant Colonel John Spaulding of the Office of the Secretary of the Air Force replied to their letters. He offered the following pithy consolation: "Based on additional information submitted to our UFO investigation officer [at] Wright-Patterson AFB, Ohio, we have been unable to identify the object you observed on September 3, 1965."

The resultant Project Blue Book report is a voluminous 131 pages and comprises typed and handwritten correspondence between officials and civilians, interoffice memos and notes, witness statements, newspaper clippings, maps, and charts. Also included are several other reports of unidentified craft from the same general area and time frame.

For example:

- Concord, August 12: A "very bright shiny object, round [in] form, flying about 1 mile high, on a westerly course, in front of a jet airplane."

- Hampton, August 25: "Two lights with no connection between them" producing a sound "like an electric motor rather than any kind of engine."
- Weare, September 4: A "single bright shining object. Brightest object in the sky, no moon visible. First seen when overhead, disappeared over horizon 3–5 minutes later."

When the report was officially closed, it was labeled in uppercase, typewritten letters as "UNIDENTIFIED."

Indeed, the incidents at Exeter remain among the most perplexing in the history of humankind's contact with unidentified flying objects—be they of a cosmic variety or a decidedly more earthly sort.

DOWN-TO-EARTH ALIENS?

The one place where you're guaranteed to encounter a UFO—not to mention entourages of little green or gray men, Bigfoot, and many other "out-of-this-world" artifacts and oddities—is at the Exeter UFO Festival. The event converges on Exeter's downtown every September to mark the anniversary of the strange, headline-abducting incidents there in 1965.

Local writer and self-described UFO enthusiast Dean Merchant—or simply, "the UFO guy"—first envisioned the festival and developed it with the Exeter Area Kiwanis Club (to which he belongs). Launched in 2009, it serves as a fund-raiser for the club's various charitable programs. Merchant and his fellow members have cultivated an event that is not only a must-visit for serious watchers of the skies but family-friendly, too.

For the former, it involves panel discussions, keynote presentations, and meet-and-greets; for the latter, there are alien costume contests (both bipeds and their four-legged companions included), judged by a "genuine alien," and "crash sites" full of interstellar debris ripe for exploration. Meanwhile, trolley tours run on a regular loop, taking festivalgoers of all types to the site of the incident along State Route 150.

According to organizers, hundreds of spectators have crowded the downtown area and assembled in the historic town hall to hear about first-person encounters; theories of cover-ups or joint military/alien abductions; the process of independent and official government investigations; and expert research on crop circles, Bigfoot, paranormal entities, and other mysterious forces.

Particularly when it comes to the Granite State, aliens "seem to be very curious about our use of nuclear things," Merchant told *New Hampshire Magazine.*

And that abiding curiosity indeed goes both ways.

THE HILL ABDUCTION

Is it . . . is it *chasing* us?

These were among the many frantic thoughts shared by Betty and Barney Hill as they sped through the White Mountains in September 1961, purportedly pursued by aggressive, unexplainable lights.

The husband and wife had just wanted to get away for a few days. Little did they know that their spur-of-the-moment delayed honeymoon would result in lost blocks of time and other inexplicable phenomena; startling nightmares, repressed memories, and numerous psychiatric sessions; a US Air Force investigation; and a media firestorm. Their accounts (both conscious and subconscious) of that night would become one of the most infamous alien abduction experiences in history.

An otherwise quiet and unassuming biracial couple, Betty was a welfare case worker and Barney pulled night shifts at the post office. The pair devoted what free time they had to their church and activities related to the civil rights movement. In September 1961 they set off on their trip through Montreal and Niagara Falls, traveling with their dachshund, Delsey. On the last night of their three-day trip, September 19, the couple planned to drive straight through from Vermont to Portsmouth. They wanted to beat some bad weather that was coming in ahead of an approaching hurricane.

Barney guided their '57 Chevrolet Bel Air along the winding, at times precipitous, US Highway 3 through the White Mountains. It was dark, far past midnight but nowhere near dawn. The mountains crowded the road in ominous silhouettes; the pair had seen no other cars or signs of human life for miles.

Suddenly, Betty saw a bright spot of light. Just a falling star, Barney said. But it dallied, not disappearing or fading—in fact, it grew larger and brighter. It had come from below the moon and below Jupiter, Betty said. Most likely a satellite that had gone off course, Barney assured his wife. Nothing to worry about.

But as it continued to grow in size and luminosity—and became increasingly aggressive—such assurances were ever more difficult to make. It didn't move like a regular plane or jet; it was too fast to be a weather balloon, too quiet to be a helicopter. And the experience was going on far too long for it to be some kind of optical illusion.

The light zoomed in and out, zigging and zagging, dipping out of sight behind hills and ridges, reappearing moments later. All the while, it kept up right along with the Chevy, never disappearing from sight for more than a few seconds. Looking at it with binoculars, Betty exclaimed that it was some kind of craft that was spinning, oddly shaped, and flashing multicolored lights.

After several long minutes of toying with the couple, the object rapidly descended toward their car. Barney braked to a halt as it bobbed about 100 feet away. As big as a jet but round and flat like a pancake, it dominated their field of vision.

Barney grabbed a gun he kept hidden beneath the seat and jumped out of the car. He raised the binoculars, gasped, and whispered, "This can't be real."

Through rows of windows, he claimed to see several gray "somehow not human" figures looking back at him. They wore glossy black uniforms and black caps. Frozen, Barney felt—rather than heard—one of them telling him to stay where he was and to keep looking.

That shocked him out of his trance. They were going to be captured! Hysterically, he ran back to the car, jumped in, and sped off. By then the craft had rapidly closed in, hovering directly above them. Betty stuck her head out the window and looked up.

Without explanation—which, really, it all was at this point—loud, rhythmic buzzes or beeps emanated from the area of the trunk. The car vibrated; the couple felt tingly and then were absorbed in a cloaking drowsiness.

Another series of bangs and high-pitched whistles returned both of them to consciousness.

It seemed that only seconds had passed—but it was nearly two hours later, and they had somehow traveled 35 miles farther south.

All that either of them could recall about the time or distance was that they had encountered a sudden roadblock; turning away from it, they saw a fiery orb hovering in the middle of the road. That's it. Neither of them remembered anything else.

Exhausted, shocked, they continued, arriving at their Portsmouth home as dawn was starting to transform the landscape into hazy silhouettes. They felt disheveled and dirty. Their watches had stopped working. Barney's shoes were scuffed; Betty's dress was ripped. And there were shiny, concentric circles on the car's trunk.

They inspected themselves, showered, and napped fitfully; made sketches; inspected their clothes, luggage, and car; experimented with a compass (it whirled when getting anywhere near the circles on the trunk).

On the 21st, Betty called Pease Air Force Base to make a report. They talked with Major Paul W. Henderson, who suggested that they had "misidentified" Jupiter. His report was then forwarded to Project Blue Book, which launched an investigation.

Meanwhile, Betty had a series of five vivid dreams involving little men, probing procedures, and excruciating pain. Barney, usually pragmatic and cautious, had become anxious and edgy. Exploring the notion of UFOs, Betty borrowed several books from the library, learning about and eventually writing to the civilian group the National Investigations Committee on Aerial Phenomena (NICAP). The couple also sought psychiatric help, agreeing to undergo hypnosis with psychiatrist and neurologist Benjamin Simon.

Through several sessions, each conducted separately, Simon plumbed the depths of their subconscious minds, revealing disturbing details from their unaccounted-for hours.

Initially fearful, incredulous, and at times yelling out, Barney recalled that, once the car was stopped, six of the humanoid creatures disembarked from the craft, forcing him and Betty to walk through the forest, then up a ramp into the disc-shaped craft.

The beings were gray, with large, mesmerizing eyes; bluish lips; and dark hair, according to both Betty and Barney. They stood about five feet tall and wore matching black uniforms and caps.

Once inside the ship, the husband and wife were separated. Their clothes were removed, and they each took a turn lying on a cold silver table in a sparse examination room. Barney described a cuplike device that was placed over his genitals and a cylinder that was inserted quickly into his anus. Betty recalled that a large needle, about half a foot long, was stuck into her navel (some sort of pregnancy test, she thought), causing extreme pain. The "men" also scraped off skin cells, peered into the humans' eyes and mouths, counted their vertebrae, and took clippings of their hair and nails.

All the while, the beings mumbled—although their mouths never seemed to move. Barney said he couldn't understand them, while Betty claimed she could at times. Throughout the ordeal, she described individuals in the group such as "the leader" and "the examiner." She actually had a conversation with the leader, she claimed. When she asked where the craft had flown from, she was told that there wasn't any point in telling her due to her acknowledged ignorance of the universe. Under hypnosis, however, she would draw a star map she claimed to have been shown while on the ship. Upon later analysis by independent researchers, it seemed to distinctly resemble the Zeta Reticuli star system (located about 39 light-years from Earth).

Finally, when the beings were done with their tests, Betty and Barney both recalled being led back to their car and reawakened from their trance—where their conscious memories resumed.

The psychiatrist would later say that he never felt the Hills were implicitly lying; he concluded that it was a fantasy inspired by Betty's initial vivid dreams—which Barney had "absorbed." Meanwhile, the couple revisited the site several times in hopes of sparking further memories or sensations and were interviewed by both NICAP and Project Blue Book examiners. NICAP concluded that their story was credible; the federal agency was more dismissive.

The 57-page Project Blue Book report includes witness testimony, newspaper clippings, and several pages of weather charts and adiabatic (thermodynamic) formulas.

As summed up by investigators, the couple encountered a "continuous band of light, cigar-shaped at all times despite changes of direction. Described as "V"-shaped with red lights on tips. Wings seemed to suddenly appear from [its] main body. Later, wings appeared to extend further. Varied directions abruptly and disappeared to north."

Ultimately, the report notes "inconsistencies" in the husband's and wife's accounts, while there were "no specific details on maneuverability" given, no lateral or vertical movement indicated, and "the actual light source is not known." Although the case was ultimately closed and labeled "Insufficient data for analysis," reviewers pointed to a "strong inversion which prevailed in the area on the morning of the sighting" and said that the light "has all the characteristics of an advertising search light." Jupiter was also setting to the southwest at the approximate time that the object appeared. "There is no evidence indicating [that the] objects were due to anything other than natural causes," the report concludes. "The object was in all probability Jupiter."

The couple maintained a low profile for a time, telling friends, members of their church group, and interested UFO researchers about their encounter. That was until October 1965, when they were pulled into the media's tractor beam. On October 25, the newspaper *Boston Traveler* published an account of their story with the headline: "UFO Chiller: Did THEY Seize Couple?" The story was picked up by United Press International (UPI), and writer John G. Fuller approached them about a book collaboration. The result was the bestseller *The Interrupted Journey*, published in 1966.

In the 50-plus years since, their account has been analyzed down to the minutest detail, featured in countless articles, research papers, theses, and books. They have likewise been portrayed and referenced in graphic novels, movies, and TV shows, including the 1975 TV adaptation *The UFO Incident* starring James Earl Jones and Estelle Parsons, *The X-Files*, Carl Sagan's *Cosmos* miniseries, and *American Horror Story*.

The state officially recognized the couple in 2011 with a marker outside the Indian Head Resort in Lincoln. Betty's alma mater, the University of New Hampshire, maintains an extensive archive, including correspondence, personal history, notebooks, journals, publications, news clippings, photographs, artwork, and even Betty's dress from that night. The location of their "abduction" has also been combed, explored, and combed again; one private collector even claims to have a piece of metallic material that dripped off something that hovered above the site, cooling and hardening into a blob with a perfectly smooth top and a mottled bottom.

Over the years, despite public ridicule, ribbing, and outright hostility, the couple remained steadfast in their story. Barney didn't live long enough to see himself portrayed on celluloid; he died in 1969 at age 46 of a brain aneurism. Betty lived to be 85; she passed away in 2004 from lung cancer.

"Betty and Barney had the opinion that they just happened to be in the right place at the right time, or you could say the *wrong* time," said their niece, Kathleen Marden, who went on to become a noted ufologist, penning, among other books, *Captured: The Betty and Barney Hill Experience*.

She was 13 at the time of the incident and claims, "I saw the spots. I held the watches. I believe it is more than coincidence," she asserts.

Whether coincidence or divined, truth or fiction, fantasy or reality, the Hill case has captivated believers, agnostics, and atheists alike since that fateful night in 1961.

THE BOOMERANG EFFECT

It wasn't just a one-off, flit-in-the-sky sighting. In September and October 2014, people from Manchester to Keene, Amherst to Milford, spotted the weird, brightly lit, boomerang-shaped "craft."

One of the first to catch a glimpse of it—and a picture, too—was teenager Ben Speigel. While hanging out with friends in his north-end Concord neighborhood around 8:00 p.m. on October 5, he looked up to see a brightish orb in the sky with something like a helicopter in pursuit. It was "V"-shaped, and he was clear about the fact that it wasn't blinking like a plane is likely to do. "It was zig-zagging across the sky, not fast, but it kept going back and forth," he told the *Huffington Post*. "It made a turn and went up and then down and then back and forth again. As it was circling around, it went up and circled again."

Naturally, Speigel took out his phone and grabbed some snaps of the object before it shot off behind some trees. In those images, a fuzzy "V" shape can be seen in stark contrast to a black night sky.

About a half-hour later and to the south, in the border town of Nashua, the Bowe family had their encounter with "it." They were driving along the Everett Turnpike, which traverses the lower half of the state north to south, when they sighted something bright, big, and floating hundreds of feet above the ground. Because he was driving about 50 miles an hour, Bowie estimated that it was going no faster than 30 or 40, gliding above the treetops. At one point he lost sight of it; then it came back into view.

One of the most striking things was how it was illuminated: "The lights on this thing were perfectly round and shaped like domes," he asserted. They were located at its nose and at the end of each of its "wings." His wife added that she saw amber colors on each tip, as well. None of the lights blinked; they appeared steady and constant.

Bowe stressed that he'd lived in Nashua for more than 20 years and was well acquainted with the flight paths of the small public-use Nashua Airport.

But this? Definitely not a plane, he said. Among its other characteristics, it simply seemed to move according to its own rules, at times defying the laws of physics. In one spectacular maneuver, it turned at a 90-degree angle at "extremely low speed, altitude, and without sound," he said. "Any plane would have dropped from the sky at the speed this was going."

Not to mention, he would have clearly seen marker and landing lights had it been a traditional plane.

Once he got home, Bowe contacted Nashua Airport to see if they could provide flight logs. He said he received an e-mail response stating that there was no air traffic at that time, and no one was on duty. He filed a report with the Mutual UFO Network (MUFON), who turned the case over to New Hampshire field investigator Mark Podell. He told reporters that all the indicators pointed to it being a man-made object, "possibly stealth aircraft that has abilities that most people are not aware of." Others agreed that it could have been a stealth fighter or military jet.

In any case, it was startling enough that other locals reported seeing it above Manchester, Concord, Pittsfield, Amherst, Keene, and Milford, according to the local Patch.com news site. Several of them sent in sketches and photos, including a resident of Boscawen, who claimed to see the object several days later, on October 11. These images show a startlingly white boomerang-shaped object above the top reaches of leafless trees against a blue sky; what looks like a reverse, uncoiling "S" composed of seven bright lights; and a sketch of a "V" with three circles representing lights at its apex and two tails.

Bowe went so far as to work with a graphic artist to come up with some sketches; his son also created a 3-D model. These representations show a smooth, streamlined, futuristic triangle. It is jet black, traced with horizontal and zigzagging lines, and equipped with three lights—one at each of its points.

Speigel, for his part, doesn't venture to guess. "I didn't know what to think," he shrugged. "It was just there."

Bowe's opinion? It wasn't a blimp. It wasn't a drone. "I think it was extraterrestrial," he asserted.

The answer, though, seems to remain beyond the stars and out of reach.

CONFIRMED PROOF?

It plays like a clip from a video game: A jet scope has a black spherical object targeted in its sights—whirling, darting, rotating to keep up with it over banks of billowy clouds.

But, in fact, this was a real-life flying saucer.

It was captured in 2004 as part of a "real-world tasking" mission involving Windham resident David Fravor and became public in late 2017 after the Pentagon publicly acknowledged the existence of a recent, five-year-long secret program dedicated to studying unidentified flying objects.

"It was a real object, it exists, I saw it," Fravor told the *Washington Post*, describing it as "something not from this Earth."

The retired pilot encountered that "something" while leading a US Navy strike fighter squadron of F/A-18 Hornet fighter planes on November 14, 2014. Flying about 60 to 100 miles off the coast of San Diego, the squad was performing a training exercise in advance of a deployment to the Persian Gulf.

Then Command radioed in. They were to suspend their operation and head 60 miles west for some "real-world tasking."

(Real world? Or out of this world?) They were notified that several unidentified flying objects had been tracked in that area over the last several weeks. They were all similar and followed the same relative pattern, descending from 80,000 feet to 20,000 feet then disappearing.

Fravor led his team in, and they quickly spotted the strange object, flying below around a patch of whitewater.

He described it as a "40-foot-long Tic Tac with no wings," recalling that it created no rotor wash, the visible air turbulence left by the blades of a helicopter.

As they approached and began pursuing it, the object moved around randomly—north, south, east, west, "just stopping, going the other direction, like you could do with a helicopter, but a little bit more abrupt," Fravor explained.

And then? "As I get closer, as my nose is starting to pull back up, it accelerates and it's gone. Faster than I'd ever seen anything in my life."

It wasn't below them, above them, anywhere around them. It just vanished.

Shortly after, Fravor's plane headed back to the USS *Nimitz* aircraft carrier for docking. A separate crew had been dispatched to look for the object—and, either locating the same craft or a similar unidentified craft, tracked it and shot the now-viral video.

Fravor said he was not ordered to keep it quiet. His superiors knew; everyone on the jet knew. After he retired from the Navy in 2006, he shared the story with his family and assorted friends. But he really didn't give it much thought, and nothing really came of it—even after he received a call in 2009 from a government official (whom he declined to name) who claimed to be doing "an unofficial investigation."

He later learned that the encounter was analyzed by the Defense Department program, but the questions of what exactly it was and what it was doing still remain unanswered.

Fravor has no idea, and doesn't venture to guess or theorize. But he is intrigued and exhilarated by the possibilities.

"This is revolutionary technology," he said of the craft and its capabilities. "Think about the advances that would bring to mankind. What if it actually starts to get people to think outside the box?"

The box—or the Earth?

PROJECT BLUE BOOK FILES

In the 22-year period that the federal government investigated claims of unidentified flying objects through its Project Blue Book program, roughly 40 of those originated in New Hampshire (this includes formal reports looking into both the incident at Exeter and the Betty and Barney Hill abduction). Those outlined here were deemed to have no known origin, or the details presented were "insufficient" for reviewers to come to a definitive conclusion. The discretion is the reader's.

On September 14, 1947, in Lebanon, a beekeeper "rather intently" watching her honeybees suddenly spotted a saucer and a ball-shaped object moving together in the sky. The ball appeared first, floating above the bee box; it was "as large as a tennis ball" and as "white as cotton batting." It approached "rapidly and noiselessly" from the east, followed by another object that appeared saucer-shaped. This larger object maintained a constant angle of inclination to the ball and followed it at a constant distance. "The two objects made

an angle with my eye of approximately five degrees," the witness wrote. "They were in my vision for more than a minute when I lost them in the glare of the sun."
Conclusion: None given.

On July 24, 1951, in Portsmouth, two military personnel witnessed an unusual object flying over US Highway 1. A captain and a corporal from Hanscom Air Force Base (located west of Boston) said that the craft had a shape "like a long tube with a fin construction on one end" and was between 100 and 200 feet long. Its thickness was about one-fifth its length, they estimated. Most curiously, it resembled "fused glass, being grayish to invisible in color," and its entire surface was "covered with black polka-dotted spots." The object traveled from east to west above the toll bridge the captain and corporal were driving across, going at least 800 miles an hour at an elevation of 1,000 feet or higher. It created no discernible sound and left no exhaust or vapor trail, "except a swath like a very weak rainbow." It was in view for about 20 seconds before disappearing "very quickly," as though it had gone into a cloud bank (although no clouds were present).

"Although I could make no estimate regarding the speed of the object, I can say that it was traveling at a considerably greater rate of speed than any other type of aircraft that I have ever seen," the corporal said in a statement. "Although the object was not well defined, its shape resembled that of a large hot dog, tapering slightly toward the rear and perhaps four or five times as long as it was high."
Conclusion: "Unidentified."

On May 31, 1954, in Concord, a white elongated object was witnessed going at an "unbelievable" speed. "It was very long and narrow," the observer reported, noting that it traveled in a "perfectly straight line" directly in front of her and then seemed to be "falling straight down." "It had a strange whiteness about it, as the sky was a dark grayish blue, which made it stand out so plain," she said. It was in view for between 8 and 10 seconds; then it simply vanished—not getting smaller or farther away or moving out of sight. "It disappeared while *still* a large object," the observer wrote, " so that it gave me a queer feeling."
Conclusion: "Unidentified."

On September 5, 1956, in Concord, witnesses reported seeing "three objects three times the size of a star" that were bright and "almost luminous." They moved up and fast and could easily be differentiated from traditional aircraft in the sky.
Conclusion: "Motion upward indicates possible balloon; however, no data to substantiate this conclusion. Insufficient data for evaluation."

On November 7, 1957, in Manchester, observers reported a "round object, size of grapefruit, red and white. [Followed] very irregular path. Faded." When it was in sight, they added, the electricity in the house went out.
Conclusion: "Possible aircraft sighting."

On February 2, 1958, in Ashland, witnesses claimed to spot "thirty bright lights massed in a group" with bursts of fire at the reach of each. They appeared to be in no particular design or formation. When in view, they "interfered" with the television set.

Conclusion: "No duration, size, shape, or color of objects; no description of maneuvers or flight path. No data for analysis."

On May 20, 1960, in Jaffrey Center, an observer spotted a strange object crossing the span of their bedroom window. The "clear-cut circle or disc" was plainly visible, "very bright and deep gold, about three times as large as a planet, size similar to the sun seen high through thick clouds." It appeared to be descending, moving diagonally from the top sightline of the window (east) to the bottom (west). "I was unquestionably wide awake," the witness stated. "I was so much impressed by the object that I at once awakened my husband."

Investigators pointed out that had the object been a balloon, it would not have crossed the area covered by the window so rapidly; while, on the other hand, an aircraft would undoubtedly have crossed it much faster. They posited that it "was probably a reflection."

Conclusion: "Insufficient data for analysis."

On December 31, 1960, in Nashua, a viewer reported an object in the sky over their neighborhood that was "saucer-shaped, dull, and silver gray and making a sound like a small motorboat." It came to their attention because it reflected a bright flash of light, they reported. When it finally disappeared, it simply climbed straight up into the clouds.

"Dear Sirs: I just saw a flying saucer, first time in my life with my own eyes," the witness wrote. "I've read of it in newspapers, seen pictures of it in movie news. But nothing like this one." They concluded that they were not mistaken on that fact: "The flying saucer I've seen today was no play toy from somebody's backyard. I'm sure."

Conclusion: "Insufficient data for evaluation." "The cause of this sighting was probably a reflection, mirage, or both."

———

Between May 27 and May 29, 1962, in Troy, several witnesses saw a bright object flying low on the horizon shortly after sunset. It appeared to be moving up and down and sideways. One witness claimed that the object disappeared at one point to be "replaced by six objects." One observer wrote that "this look[ed] like the Unidentified Flying Objects that some of the servicemen in the Army took pictures of."

Conclusion: "Insufficient data for evaluation." "The planets Venus and Jupiter are probably the prime culprits."

———

On October 23, 1963, in New Hampton, witnesses reported an irregular blinking object, ivory white, like "the reflection of gold in dim light." As it crossed the western sky, it seemed to be followed by an identical light.

Conclusion: "Inconsistences in report. Case carried as conflicting data."

———

On February 26, 1966, in Bartlett, three observers reported a bright round object "not as big as the moon" coming toward them out of the east. It appeared "bright white fluorescent light–like," with a red glow all around it and a dark area at its center. Over a course of roughly 10 minutes, it grew brighter and dimmer, appearing and disappearing three different times. The trio of witnesses included a husband and wife, who reported that their dog was highly disturbed by the incident—and, in fact, had been "uneasy" all evening leading up to the encounter. The investigator described the observers as "farm people who are not very articulate when it comes to description of things." As such, they provided "woefully meager" bits of information.

The writer of the ensuing report marveled that the wife shook the husband awake and exclaimed, "There is a flying saucer in the yard!" The investigator then marveled that "this sort of statement occurs quite frequently and indicates how readily people [of] all walks of life seem to accept the existence of flying saucers and . . . that they are not too startled when they apparently see one!"
Conclusion: "Possible aircraft—but not possible to say much more because of indeterminate nature of report."

On July 25, 1967, in Manchester, a driver traveling through a residential area spotted a peculiar object that had a brightness like "a steel bar when heated with a torch." Its edges were sharply outlined, it was predominantly red with a whitish highlight, and it didn't seem to generate any sound. The craft was about 1,000 feet above the ground, the witness estimated, and it faded away as though traveling at a very high speed. "I took special care in its movement and its shape," he reported, emphasizing that he knew the terrain very well. "I checked the area completely for other aircraft." To bolster his credibility, he added, "I do not drink. I am a local businessman dealing in custom homes. Whenever anything unusual happens to me, I do not get excited. I try to notice every detail that may be of importance."
Conclusion: "Possible aircraft/with advertising sign."

On November 4, 1967, in Hanover, an observer reported a black object zooming over the roof of his car. It was five feet in diameter, three feet thick, and came within five feet of the top of his vehicle, he estimated. It made no noise but had a distinct smell "like ozone." The object "gave off gas vapors and smoke" and was "like a fogbank," according to the witness, who identified himself as a father and employed at Thermal Dynamics Corporation in West Lebanon.

The report's investigator summed up his findings: "Nothing unusual was reported on radar; nothing unusual was reported to local police; also nothing unusual as to air traffic in area." **Conclusion:** "Insufficient data for evaluation."

On January 16, 1968, in Canaan, an observer reported a dark, lead-colored object drifting low across the sky. Seen through a 20-power telescope, it had the "appearance of a short section of a sheet iron mill stack." It traversed such a slow path that it almost had no perceptible movement, the witness explained, and from its top, a narrow line of what looked like coal smoke extended to the northwest horizon, "perfectly straight and against the strong wind." Meanwhile, its surface looked like an "old-time, dirty hot air balloon with a somewhat mottled surface like a toad." It drifted away—then, suddenly, it reappeared several minutes later at its original starting point. Only this time it was "inverted, the smoke column pouring out of the bottom and heading southwest with the strong wind," the observer marveled. "How it had returned against the wind was more than I could understand." He added (rather poetically) that the bizarre object continued to stand "amid the wind-torn clouds, looking somewhat distorted until darkness shut out the view."

Conclusion: "Insufficient data for evaluation."

FISHING CAN BE A BONDING EXPERIENCE

It was near dark; the two young fishermen were on the lookout for horned pout (a type of catfish) at their favorite fishing spot in Hopkinton. There had been no significant bites yet, so they lingered a little longer than usual, lighting a Coleman lantern both to see by and to (hopefully) attract some fish.

Suddenly, as one of the witnesses would later recall of that night in July 1976, an odd object whirred in above the lake. Alarmed, the teenagers switched off their lantern and "observed with a combination of fear and awe."

The thing, definitely a craft of some sort, passed over them at altitude of less than 200 feet. It was triangular—25 to 30 feet wide at its widest, 3 or 4 feet wide at its narrowest—and had a half-dozen or so rectangular lights at its belly that rotated and changed color. "The very rear of the craft looked strikingly similar to the taillights of a 1965 Ford Galaxy," the witness recalled on a UFO-reporting website.

As it moved slowly over the water, it made a "very low bass frequency sound"—kind of like a jet when it's idling or warming up. That sound continued to increase as the object passed directly overhead, then halted and hovered over the middle of the lake. At that point, it was about 150 feet or so above the water and 500 away from the fishermen, who sat slack-jawed and hunkering in their boat under the canopy of an overhanging tree. "We had a clear and unobstructed view," the witness wrote. "The moonlight illuminated the surroundings well enough to see the landscape . . . and to see with decent detail the shapes and colors of the craft."

It was aluminum (or at least aluminum in color) and had a narrow band of lights flanking its entire right side. Those glowed a "very high intensity," like LED lights (which of course didn't exist at the time), "but even brighter, like a welder's arc."

Suddenly, a narrow beam of white light shot out of the bottom of the triangle and swirled several times in a circular motion. Then it was extinguished, and the low humming sound began to wind up, like a propulsion system was turning on. The craft then angled up, its rear lights glowing a "very bright, then an almost plasma-like glow"—and it shot off with incredible speed into the sky.

Just as soon as it had materialized, it was gone.

The fishermen remained where they were, expectantly; then, as the night grew cooler and darker, they lifted their oars and headed back for shore, both perplexed and exhilarated.

Neither of the teenagers saw the object again.

So—maybe it was the bait?

MEANWHILE, IN MORE RECENT INTERGALACTIC HISTORY . . .

On November 5, 2006, in Atkinson, a witness driving along North Main Street as dark was settling in suddenly spotted two rows of peculiar light formations in the sky. One was composed of seven lights, the other nine, and they ran roughly parallel to one another. At first, the observer noted, "I thought nothing of it until I caught the way it moved." That is, with a "gentle burst of speed," the lights flew in their parallel pattern very low over the road from east to west. They could have formed a rough outline of a larger elliptical craft, the witness noted, but the formations moved so fast that there was no opportunity to (literally) "connect the dots." Could it, they wondered, have had some correlation to America's Stonehenge—a 4,000-year-old archaeological site in nearby Salem?

"I'm not a quack," the observer insisted. "I'm not a Richard Dreyfuss who's going to pile up my potatoes into the shape I saw."

⸻

On November 16, 2007, in Kingston, a husband and wife had an extended viewing of a strange object that was "moving very quickly, like a bat flapping its wings." It was around 3:30 a.m. when it first appeared, initially glowing green at its rim, then flashing to red. Like "something spinning real fast," it changed colors, expanded and shrunk, moved in and out. Then, they said, it just sat over their house in the same spot for about an hour and a half. They showed a friend who is a US Air Force pilot and relayed that he thought it was "quite unusual." "We have no explanation for the changing colors and shapes," the witness stated.

⸻

On June 20, 2007, an observer visiting the White Mountain region captured an image of an "object flying around erratically" above Mount Washington. He was standing in the parking lot of the visitor center at the beginning of the Mount Washington Auto Road (which wends its way to the top of Mount Washington's 6,288-foot summit), taking pictures of the view with his Canon PowerShot digital camera. The submitted photo appears to be just a typical shot of the mountain range in the distance; however, when blown up and zoomed, the blurry outline of a round silver object can be seen against the blue afternoon sky.

⸻

On July 31, 2014, in Milford, a viewer up at the predawn hour of 3:45 a.m. spotted a chevron-shaped object through the kitchen window. It was flying low in a northerly direction. The witness immediately ran outside to her deck to get a better look because, despite how close it seemed to be, she couldn't hear any sound. It flew above the tree line, "quite a bit lower" than the usual air traffic, and it had decidedly more lights than an airplane—about 12 or 13 altogether and all but one of them white (one red one stood out on its own). She guessed that the overall width was 70 to 100 feet. It continued to move north until drifting out of sight. "What struck me was the total silence," the witness wrote. "As low as this thing was flying, I heard nothing at all." She stressed that she had lived in the flight path of a number of airports throughout her 51 years and was "very used to air traffic." "This craft was absolutely nothing like anything I have seen," she said.

— ⁓ —

On September 21, 2015, an observer captured more than three minutes of video of an odd array of bright lights above Concord. The resulting footage, filmed by Mike Pittaro and his wife, was posted on social media and viewed more than 350,000 times. The couple caught it quite by accident: They were taking photos of the sunset and the changing hues of the night-darkening sky above a shopping plaza when they spotted the "UFOs" on their screens. "These objects were NOT visible to the naked eye," Pittaro wrote in one of the threads. Furthermore, he added, "after asking multiple people to use their cell phones, they too caught the exact same UFOs, verifying what we were recording." Some commenters claimed to have also seen the lights.

The video shows a cluster of bulbous lights that remain in relative formation high up in the sky; some break off at intervals, disappearing and reappearing. Enlarged images reveal what appear to be silver-gray shapes with rounded edges. Pittaro can be heard exclaiming, "What the heck is that? Yeah it's moving, it's above the clouds . . . oh, oh, it's changing shape!"

On December 11, 2015, a driver passing through the perilous Crawford Notch in the vicinity of the Bretton Woods area saw something "like fireballs in the sky." Described as being like "a sonic wave," it appeared in one spot, then disappeared, only to reappear seconds later in a completely different area of the sky. It moved along the top of the mountain ranges for 20 or 30 seconds, zigzagging, its lights flashing bright then extinguishing. It was orange colored, big and "fast—really fast." The witness claimed that other cars were pulled over watching, "so it wasn't me hallucinating."

On April 21, 2016, in Lincoln, a witness watched and videotaped an object that appeared to be trailing a jet. It was around 7:00 p.m., and he was out on his deck, according to "Case 81792" from the Mutual UFO Network (MUFON) witness-reporting database. The observer said he often watched military planes flying in the vicinity and that "jets and helicopters are a common sighting." So naturally, when he spotted this jet, he "did a double take" because something seemed to be following it. That "something" looked "strange"—"possibly something the military built, but not a jet." By contrast, the jet it appeared to be "chasing" left a long contrail, but it did not. Furthermore, the strange craft was gaining on the jet. "No helicopter could do that," he said. "I was blown away. I watched the object gaining on the jet for about 10 seconds when I lost them in the trees."

A 25-second-long video submitted to MUFON shows a tiny bright pinpoint in the sky, seemingly gaining speed as it crosses from right to left. Below it and (at first) ahead of it is the jet, indeed trailing a long line of vapor. The unidentified object zooms along, quickly catching up to the jet and overtaking it, then traveling parallel above it before both disappear out of sight behind a tree.

The witness then said he saw three more jets and one helicopter going in the same direction, "in my opinion chasing the UFO." "I felt I had witnessed something very hard to dismiss as a weather balloon or some obvious type of aircraft," he said. "I would like to show the video to an aviation expert and maybe get an explanation."

⸻

On March 20, 2017, in Hudson, an observer saw a "hovering, pulsating light" just above the treetops. According to "Case 82743" in the MUFON database, the witness was heading home for a lunch break at 3:45 a.m. (he works the graveyard shift) when the object caught his eye. It hovered above the parking lot of his apartment building, pulsating a "very bright white" color.

⸻

On June 21, 2017, in Keene, a witness reported two "bright reddish-orange lights" up in the sky. They were "far apart" but moving slowly at the same speed and in the same direction (relative northwest). "There was no sound or flashing," the observer said. Then one of them vanished, the second dematerializing shortly thereafter. She tried to get pictures, she said, but "of course" only got one blurry one because the camera didn't seem to function right. "That is typical!" The accompanying photo depicts a hazy red glowing blob—what looks to be triangular or boomerang-shaped—against a pitch black sky. "I have always been a skeptic about UFOs and need some kind of explanation," the witness added. "I am baffled by this one."

One commenter on the report of this alleged sighting said he spotted a similarly "huge orange-reddish orb-like craft" four days earlier, on June 17. "You could see through it, but inside it looked like orange/red smoke swirling around," the commenter wrote. "It flew pretty slow and then disappeared over the ocean."

—⁓—

On July 15, 2017, in Newton, an observer watched a "teardrop-shaped bright light" crossing the sky. It was fuzzy, according to testimony in "Case 85667" from the MUFON database. "I knew it wasn't a helicopter or anything because it was too fast," the witness stated. It was bigger, faster, and lower to the ground than a plane, probably about 1,000 feet in the air and moving in a straight line. It had a red-orange tint, was fuzzy, "strange and hard to interpret." The craft moved along in the northeastern sky in the direction of the Seabrook Nuclear Power Plant and Pease Air Force Base.

The report is accompanied by a rough sketch depicting tall sweeps of trees, the round ball of the moon, and a teardrop shape in the top left corner. "It eventually left my sight and I went to bed," the witness wrote. The case was investigated by New Hampshire MUFON state director Valerie Schultz, who eventually closed it with the conclusion that it was an "Unknown Aerial Vehicle."

—⁓—

On February 18, 2018, in Barrington, an observer sighted "10-plus orange glowing lights" moving through the sky and "making no sound whatsoever." He at first spotted just one of them as he stepped outside; it moved from east to north about 20 to 30 degrees above the horizon. "I then noticed that there was another one coming up behind it," he reported. "Then came another, and another. They just kept coming." They moved around in a shimmery cluster; one "shot down out of nowhere," stopped right on top of another, and proceeded along at the same speed.

There were no flashing lights or landing/takeoff lights, and they were too fast and agile for conventional craft. With a snow-storm coming, the sky was cloudy with a low ceiling. The objects made no sound. "In fact, it was strange how quiet it became when these were passing by," he said, adding that, after he saw them, he could hear the sound of military jet traffic emanating from Pease Air Force Base, about 20 minutes from his house.

On July 10, 2018, on Seabrook Beach, a kayaker saw a "multi-colored sphere" moving directly overhead. As it moved slowly along, it was accompanied by "a bunch of smaller red orbs mov-ing in all directions," as well as a very large triangular shape with greenish lights. The kayaker watched it for about 10 minutes until the sphere and the triangle "instantly and silently went straight up and [were] gone in less than a second."

On September 23, 2018, on Hampton Beach, a cyclist saw an unmistakable line of red orbs along the horizon. They were spread out across a mile, level with the low clouds, and had two tones—red and white. Although they seemed to reflect the setting sun, they definitely had their own illumination and were "clearly dis-tinguishable" from a plane and helicopter flying closer and lower in the sky. They sped along silently, proceeding in a straight line south to north at the relative speed of a single-engine aircraft. Then they turned into a cloud bank and "disappeared that way one by one."

On October 28, 2018, in Nashua, a motorist spotted a distinct boomerang-shaped craft in the sky. It had white, yellow, and red lights of different sizes and brightness; the two red lights were big and located at either end, while the others ran down the inner side of the "V" shape. It looked "thin but powerful" and was about half the length of a house. It then lowered into the trees and vanished.

Stay tuned for more, with an eye on the skies . . .

FOUR

VERMONT

Vast Wilderness, Vast Wonders

*The night sky lies so sprent with stars that there is scarcely space
of black at all and they fall all night in bitter arcs and it is so
that their numbers are no less.*

—CORMAC MCCARTHY

PICTURE THE IDYLLIC SUMMER SCENE: TWO TEENAGERS, MALE
and female, sit side by side at the end of a dock jutting out into a
lake. The girls camp they work at has been mostly cleared out on
this late afternoon—campers are away at a swim meet—so the pair
take the rare occasion to lounge and relax. They chat and gossip,
occasionally dipping their feet into the lake that glitters calmly in
the August sun.

But the lackadaisical afternoon soon takes a bizarre—and
increasingly disturbing—turn.

Right around sunset, the male teenager, "Michael," spots a
bright object in the sky that he at first thinks is Venus. Soon
enough, though, he abandons that idea. The light is growing larger,
coming closer, and making marked movements—it is undulating,

in fact. He makes sure his friend "Janet" is watching, too, and what unfolds is a spectacular aerial light show that soon involves several zigzagging, spiraling, fluttering, falling, and climbing lights.

Suddenly, one of the objects appears to lock in on them; it descends low above the lake and approaches the dock.

What transpired next—lasting for an indefinite period that was many minutes or even hours, they can't be sure—on that August day in 1968 would eventually come to be known as the "Buff Ledge Abduction," one of the most vividly detailed alleged close encounters of the third kind in the history of UFO tracking and research. The five-year probe into the incident by ufologist Walter N. Webb also made it one of the most thoroughly investigated and documented of any single "abduction" episode.

With an official resident headcount hovering around 620,000, Vermont is the second-least-populated state in the United States (behind Wyoming). However, data indicates that the Green Mountain State has the most UFO sightings per capita. (Yes, really!) Based on analysis of government databases by Cheryl Costa and Linda Miller Costa in their *UFO Sightings Desk Reference*, Vermont has the most reported UFO sightings per 100,000 people.

Indeed, reports are plentiful and varied across the state and over the years, ranging from fleeting sightings far off in the night sky to full-fledged claimed abductions.

With its serene rurality, rustic mountain peaks, and acres of pristine open space and woodland, Vermont has an enigmatic quality—perhaps for the otherworldly as well?

THE INCIDENT AT BUFF LEDGE

It was their first opportunity all summer for some downtime, and Michael and Janet took full advantage.

They had no idea just how incredible that downtime would turn out to be.

The date: August 7, 1968. The setting: a private summer girl's camp on Lake Champlain north of Burlington. Sixteen-year-old Michael, from Burlington, worked for the summer maintaining waterfront equipment and ferrying water-skiers back and forth to a launching raft. Janet, a 19-year-old college student, was the water-skiing instructor.

It being late in the summer, the swim team was away in Burlington for a two-day, end-of-the-season state invitational meet. Many of the other campers and counselors took the opportunity to take overnight trips in the area. Michael and Janet—pseudonyms ascribed by Walter N. Webb, who extensively researched the case—spent most of the day swimming and lounging on the camp's "L"-shaped dock that jutted 100 feet or so into the lake.

After Michael spotted the "bright starlike object" that he at first took for Venus, the two watched, fascinated, as it swooped down out of the southwest sky in a long arc, then blossomed into a glowing white cigar shape. After coming to a complete stop, it emitted three tiny white lights; then it "vanished in seconds," while the trio of satellite lights remained.

The lights dipped and dived in the sky, growing ever closer. As they did, Michael could make them out more clearly as domed discs. Soon they formed a "horizontal triangle"; then two of them flew off in opposite directions, north and south, while the third began advancing across the lake toward the observers.

As Webb wrote later, "Michael's curiosity and awe turned to foreboding."

A colored band of light exhibiting hues "across the spectrum" rotated around the disc's edge; this seemed to pulsate in synchronization with a complex sound emission of varied tones and pitches.

Erratically, the disc shot straight up out of sight then plunged down just as quickly into the lake, triggering a steady wind and strong wave action. But it soon reemerged, gliding quickly toward the dock and pausing about 60 feet away and 15 feet up. Michael marveled that it was "as big as a small house," 40 to 50 feet wide and shaped like "two curved saucers placed face to face."

Even more incredibly, he claimed to now see a transparent dome exposing two entities. They were short creatures, large-headed and oval-eyed, with two nasal openings and small mouths. They seemed to be wearing gray or silver uniforms.

Michael glanced quickly at Janet, who seemed to be "frozen in a trance-like state," then quickly looked back. One of the human-oid beings seemed to exactly mimic her state and expression, while the other, he purported, communicated with him telepathically, relaying the fact that they were from a distant planet, their race had made earlier visits to Earth (including after the first nuclear explosions in 1945), and that he would not be harmed.

At the same time, the craft proceeded closer, coming to within about 10 feet of the witnesses. Suddenly it flashed a brilliant beam of light on them; Michael grabbed Janet and covered her protectively. He began to feel himself losing consciousness, he said, while also having the sensation of floating up, hearing machinelike noises and voices, and seeing "soft lights in a dark place" at the hazy edges of his vision.

Abruptly he came to—the disc was still hovering overhead, but it was now completely dark.

Michael could hear voices and the slamming of car doors: The campers had returned from the meet. Two of them, "Susan" and "Barbara," both 15, ran down to the bluff, crying out. Seemingly reacting to this intrusion, the craft rose, directed its beam across the camp in a rapid-fire sequence of flashes, doused the light, angled upward, and disappeared from sight. All of this occurred "in a matter of seconds," according to Michael.

He helped his dazed companion off the dock, and the two girls led her to her cabin, where she slept for some time. Michael attempted to talk with her at least once, but he was reminded that her cabin was off-limits to boys. The two later crossed paths, but thinking she might be too traumatized and not knowing exactly how to broach the subject, he said nothing.

The camp closed for the season a few weeks later, and the two went their ways. While Michael claimed to have mental flashbacks and vivid dreams, he stayed silent on the purported encounter after initially mentioning it to his family and his girlfriend, who laughed and scoffed in disbelief.

Ten years passed.

It was then that Webb, who had been a principal investigator on the legendary Barney and Betty Hill abduction in New Hampshire in 1961, decided to take up the case (publishing his results in his book *Encounter at Buff Ledge: A UFO Case History*). The enterprising researcher was able to track down both of the main "participants," as well as the two then-15-year-old girls and a third potential witness.

Michael and Janet had not had contact of any kind in the 10-plus years since the incident. To ensure that they didn't pollute or influence each other's stories, Webb interviewed them separately. They also underwent Minnesota Multiphasic Personality Inventory (MMPI) tests; psychological stress evaluator (PSE) exams; as well as background character checks that included character references and looked at their families, education, and job histories. Webb likewise determined the meteorological conditions and celestial body positions for the date, time, and place; took measurements and photographs; created maps and drawings; and even reenacted the sighting at the very location it was purported to have happened.

He also subjected the two to hypnosis—under which the story became even more detailed and bizarre.

Michael's Account

While in a trance, Michael was brought back to the moment when he and Janet were bathed in the beam of light on the dock, the ship directly overhead. He recalled becoming weak and feeling "filled with light." He also described an intense pressure and the sensation of floating up while being surrounded by streams of approaching colored lights and an increasingly loud whining sound.

Then, he claims, he found himself standing beside one of the alien entities in the transparent dome; there were screens and consoles, and streams of dim spectral lights emanated throughout the "ship." He could clearly see Earth, the Moon, the stars, and a "huge cigar-shaped craft" through the dome, he said—and then, looking down to a lower deck, he witnessed Janet lying on a rectangular table, two of the humanoid creatures examining her. Nearby was a panel filled with screens that seemed to be receiving live-feed video of the process. This array was monitored by a third creature.

According to the witness, the beings were about five to five and a half feet tall and had large, elongated heads with oval eyes and "big, round, black, shiny pupils." Their noses were simply two distinct holes, and their mouths, thin, tiny slits. They didn't appear to have ears. Long-limbed and thin, they were equipped with three-fingered, webbed hands; their skin was a "greenish-blue," and they wore dark, "greenish," skintight clothing.

Michael recalled being led by his guide down a set of stairs to the area where Janet was being poked and prodded. They shone a light in her eyes, scraped her skin, took what seemed to be a blood sample with a syringe-like instrument, and "sucked" fluids from her through two long flexible tubes. Expressing particular alarm at the latter procedure, Michael claimed that his guide reassured him telepathically that they were "spawning consciousness." (As Webb questioned in his report, could this have been the removal of ova for reproductive purposes?)

The boy then agreed to be led to another table next to Janet's; it tilted to "receive his body" then returned to a horizontal position. As the pair of examiners approached, he lost consciousness, retaining no memory, consciously or unconsciously, of his own "exam."

When he next came to, he was still lying on the table. The dome overhead was dark; the ship had apparently docked in the larger one because, as Michael rose, he and his creature guide "floated," tugged through a tube of light, into an enormous area that seemed to be a hangar. He was then whisked upward and led to a large domed room filled with several of the oval-eyed beings. A "helmet-like device" was placed on his head, and his designated watcher touched hands with his own.

This contact thrust forth images of a "strange landscape" that contained trees, grass, fountains, a "purple sky"—and suddenly a crying, frightened Janet appeared next to him. Then, just as abruptly, he was falling through space "toward a globe of many TV-like screens, like the facets in a fly's eye." All the screens displayed the same picture: the two teenagers sprawled out with the UFO above them.

It was then that Michael came to on the dock. Janet lay beside him.

Before the craft finally flew off, he claims he received a final telepathic message from his alien interpreter: "He was not to worry about the experience—nothing bad had happened to him; they were friends and cared about him; there would be much about the experience that he would not understand; and Janet would remember nothing." He was also reassured that Janet was all right. As the ship flew off, he received a final farewell: "Goodbye, Michael."

Janet's Account

According to Webb, Janet retained hardly any conscious memory of the event—beyond the fact that she and Michael were on the dock and witnessed a display of moving lights and the close approach of a "big light." Beyond that, she drew a blank.

During her regression, however, she described something "like a spaceship" that dropped "like a falling star" and approached the dock. Her description was similar to Michael's: It was a glowing, white, flat oval, "larger than a car or house," encircled with lights and emanating a high-pitched sound. Before being illuminated by a bright beam, she recalled "more than one" alien figure with "unusual heads" looking down at her from the craft.

In her next "recovered" memory, she was aboard the ship, separated from Michael, "although like her associate she had no idea how the transfer was accomplished," Webb reflected. She found herself lying on a table in a circular room under a glowing transparent dome, human-like creatures surrounding her. One of them appeared to be "in charge of" her—it told her to keep her eyes closed and stay still, while also offering reassuring, telepathic thoughts.

Despite the circumstances, she recalled being in a "semiconscious relaxed state" and "remarkably calm." The tests, her guide assured her, would not hurt.

The examiners lifted and dropped her arms, inspected her long hair. She claimed to feel heat sources on her body, "small devices of some kind" attached to her head, and a "little thing" on her neck. Although she did as instructed and kept her eyes closed through most of the experience, she did gain the courage to take a peek—and, as Webb wrote, "what she glimpsed was so strange and frightening that she shut her eyes immediately." With "great reluctance," she described the creatures: lanky-limbed, big-headed, oval-eyed. Their skin was "white or unhealthy-looking," and all wore smock-like garments. According to Webb, she described the instrument monitoring panel that Michael also saw.

She didn't have much more to add, except that when her examiners left, she rose and was led along a narrow corridor by her guide. She also said she had sensed Michael's presence during the harrowing encounter and had seen him twice.

And then? She was back on the dock. She remembered nothing and was perplexed by Michael's fear and fascination over "a few lights." She also recalled feeling drained, dazed, and light-headed.

During her regression, according to the investigator, she struggled with the "incredulity" of the emerging images; to help mitigate this, he employed deep-breathing exercises. He ultimately described the young woman as a "complete skeptic."

Conclusion?

Throughout his investigation, Webb contacted 11 former counselors and 7 ex-campers, including both of the girls who had run down to the water. They independently retained "vague memories" of an unidentified object racing away from the waterfront. Each described it as silent, dark, and circular, with lights along its curved edge.

Webb contacted an additional observer, playhouse director "Elaine," who was rehearsing *Bye Bye Birdie* with her acting troupe when someone came running up shouting about lights in the sky. Her view was obscured by trees, but she said she was aware of an ethereal "silvery glow" emanating from a moving source.

As for the primary witnesses, Webb described Michael as "bright, idealistic," interested in psychic and mystical events, and leading a "creative and artistic lifestyle." Although he dropped out of college three times and worked odd jobs while banging around the country, he finally returned to college to earn his bachelor's degree in religion. At last report, he was pursuing a modeling and acting career.

Janet was "equally bright" but more "well-adjusted, confident, outgoing, and highly motivated." She followed the "straight and narrow," graduating with honors with a bachelor's degree in psychology and pursuing a brief career path before marrying and having four children.

Ultimately, she verified 70 percent of her companion's reported details outside the craft and 68 percent of his events onboard. Both accounts coincided so closely in "gross features" and in a number of subtler details, Webb noted, that "I believe the successful recovery of original memory traces (rather than fantasized or altered pseudo-memories) is strongly indicated."

Both witnesses were "honest, credible individuals" who did not perpetrate a hoax or suffer a shared hallucination or delusion, he surmised. "The probability is high, in my judgment, that Michael and Janet experienced a real external event of unknown origin," he concluded.

It's a conclusion, though, that gives rise to many more questions than it does answers.

THE "BENNINGTON TRIANGLE"?

It is said to be roamed by a "red-eyed monster" and Bigfoot-like beasts. Strange lights and sounds emanate from its dark depths. Countless people have entered it, never to be seen again. There may even be malicious rocks there that swallow men whole.

Such is some of the folklore around the "Bennington Triangle," an area in southwest Vermont near the borders of New York and Massachusetts. Its area is vaguely defined and decidedly not a triangle by any description—the name was coined by author and paranormal researcher Joseph A. Citro, presumably to correlate its mysteries to that infamous triangle in the midst of the North Atlantic. At its heart is Glastenbury Mountain, a 3,700-foot peak that is part of the 400,000-acre Green Mountain National Forest. Radiating out from there, its willowy borders are spread out to include the towns of Glastenbury, Bennington, Woodford, Shaftsbury, and Somerset.

Contributing to the lore is the fact that Glastenbury and Somerset are abandoned. Both once thrummed with logging activity, but that waned and eventually ceased altogether, and the two townships were unincorporated by a 1937 act of the state legislature. All that remains of the two ghost towns—which, some say, are fittingly home to ghosts—are crumbling stone foundations and a very tenuous footbridge.

Purportedly, stories go back to at least the late nineteenth century; some say that, long before that, natives regarded the area as "cursed," avoiding it altogether (although this can't be substantiated).

What is without a doubt is the pattern of disappearances around Glastenbury Mountain. Most notably, between 1945 and 1950, at least five people went missing in the area. All of these cases remain unsolved.

The incident that garnered the most attention was that of 18-year-old Paula Jean Welden. The Bennington College sophomore went for a day hike on the Long Trail on December 1, 1946, never to return. She was purportedly last seen by an elderly couple also on the trail, and the fact that she was dressed in red spawned a local superstition that the color brings bad luck in this southern tip of the Green Mountains. Her disappearance triggered a massive three-week search, the offering of a $5,000 reward, and assistance from the FBI. Despite the efforts, though, no trace of the student was ever found.

A year earlier, on November 12, 1945, 74-year-old Middle Rivers, an experienced hunter and fisherman with extensive knowledge of the area, vanished while guiding a hunting expedition on the Long Trail. On the return trip through the forest, he got ahead of the group—and was never seen again. A search was conducted, but all that yielded was a single rifle cartridge at the bottom of a stream.

Three years to the day that Welden inexplicably disappeared, another person vanished. This time it was the elderly James Tedford, taking a bus from Saint Albans to Bennington on December 1, 1949. A veteran and resident of the Bennington Soldiers' Home, he was last seen on the bus at the stop just before Bennington. Somewhere in between, he went missing. Upon inspection, his belongings were still in the luggage rack; an open bus timetable was all that remained on his seat.

The ensuing instance involved an eight-year-old boy. On October 12, 1950, Paul Jephson was left alone by his mother for about an hour while she tended to some pigs. When she returned, her son was nowhere to be found. Search parties set out, but nothing was ever recovered.

The only case in which remains were found was that of Frieda Langer—but not until seven months after she vanished. The 53-year-old went missing just 16 days after Jephson, on October 28, 1950. While out hiking with her cousin, she slipped at a stream crossing and wet her clothes through. Damp and wanting to change, she returned to the family campsite, telling her cousin she would catch up. When she failed to, he returned to the site and discovered that she had not been back and had not been seen by anyone. Searches ensued, but nothing turned up. Then, on May 12, 1951, her body was discovered near the Somerset Reservoir (an area that had been extensively searched). However, due to the nature of her remains, a cause of death couldn't be determined.

Besides the general geographic area and time period, there is no evidence to connect these cases. Some UFO researchers, though, believe them to be candidates for alien abductions. They point to the fact that many strange and unidentified craft, lights, and entities have been reported in the area's skies over the years. Interestingly, ufologists also correlate Bigfoot activity—of which there has been a supposed abundance in the "triangle"—with an uptick in UFO phenomena.

Ultimately, this all yields nothing more than a giant question mark. Paranormal researchers have probed the area over the years, with one researcher creating a full-length documentary exploring its enduring mysteries. The Bennington Triangle was discussed in an episode of the Discovery Channel show *Weird or What?*— hosted by William Shatner—that aired in July 2012.

Weird? Yes. What? We'll likely never know.

THERE WAS JUST SOMETHING ABOUT 1966 . . .

It was an exciting time in the United States: The country was in the thick of the Vietnam War, race riots were abundant (the Black Panthers were soon to form), Richard Speck was on a killing spree in Chicago—and on the pop culture front, miniskirts were in vogue, *Dr. Zhivago* was in theaters, and the legendary *Star Trek* original series debuted on television.

In Vermont, the year 1966 also heralded an abundance of UFO sightings and reports.

In March, a family in Castleton in Rutland County on the New York border saw three round objects hover over their dairy farm before speeding off amid "zinging sounds," according to the *Barre Montpelier Times Argus*.

Then, on April 19 in Graniteville, there were several reports of an "odorless and soundless but not shapeless" object. Two teenage boys playing baseball spotted it at dusk, describing it to newspaper reporters as "brilliant white and giving off sparks." As they watched, it made a half-circle around a rock pile in the back of the baseball field then went straight up and out of sight. When they ran to tell adults, police were called, and a sheriff's deputy came out to investigate. As he questioned the teenagers, he found that several other residents had witnessed the odd craft, according to the *Times Argus*.

Among them was 13-year-old Janice Donahue, who was playing outside with her brothers and sisters. She identified the object as large and oval-shaped, moving slowly, with white and red flashing lights that alternately dimmed and brightened. It climbed to the top of a nearby microwave tower, hovered, then disappeared behind a hill. The teenager even drew a detailed picture of the object that was published in the newspaper.

When contacted by the same news outlet nearly 50 years later, Donahue held fast to her story and then detailed another event a few days later in Barre. She accompanied her father, a Barre constable and armed forces veteran with experience in aviation, on a call to another sighting. A small crowd had gathered at the town microwave tower to watch a large, saucer-shaped object. It had windows and flashing lights and "had the approximate size of a large commercial aircraft like a 747," she told reporters. "It moved slowly over the tower, picked up speed, and continued east." A 15-year-old girl walking in the area with her brother also reported the "mysterious object." Its lights flashed blue and red, and it made a "whizzing sound like a snap in the air."

On April 20, two housewives made an official report to the US government. In a rare daytime sighting, Mrs. William Payne of Barre, talking on the phone with Mrs. Fred Wheeler, spotted an "extremely" white object outside at about 10 minutes before noon. It was floating at about treetop level and making a "vibrating motion and nervous jitters." It was longer than it was wide and looked dented, "as if it had been hit or had run into something," Wheeler said. As she watched its relatively straight trajectory, it stopped and whirled three times. Although she didn't hear anything, she added, her chickens were stirred into a ruckus.

She excitedly told Wheeler—who lived about a quarter-mile away—what she was seeing; the other woman hung up, went outside, and spotted it, too. She called the Barre-Montpelier Airport, and later that afternoon, a major with the Intelligence Division of the Plattsburgh Air Force Base phoned both women.

The Project Blue Book report describes the sighting. "Object was pie shaped, flat on top, about the size of a dime held at arm's length, white in color and appeared to have something dangling from the bottom. Object appeared to rotate while in flight. Moved from southeast to southwest to east. Made a circle and went up and down with vibrating motion. Moving fast at times. Disappeared over tree."

The investigator described the witnesses as "sincere" but "poorly oriented as to their geographical location." His conclusion: It was a weather balloon or another object "buffeted by high gusty winds"—perhaps a "lightweight saucer-shaped lid cover off a storage/refuse container?"

That same evening, Washington County Sheriff William McSheffrey saw something "bright with red and green lights" hovering over Montpelier's Hubbard Park.

That summer and fall yielded additional sightings—one that received international attention.

On November 25, in the town of Bellows Falls, located along the Connecticut River in southern Vermont, teenagers Danny Gray and Ricky Sharp saw a peculiar, doughnut-shaped object hovering in the sky. It was noiseless, black and white, had a "shiny coil" on its dome, and appeared to be about 25 feet in diameter. It hovered about 100 feet off the ground, they said. Because they were on their way to photograph a local covered bridge, the 14-year-olds had a camera with them—and the presence of mind to snap pictures.

In all, Sharp took six photos before the object zoomed out of view. When the boys returned home and excitedly told their family and friends, however, they were met with disbelief. But a journalist with the local newspaper, the *Connecticut Valley Times-Reporter*, agreed to listen to their story and even developed the film for them. On December 10, a picture was printed in the paper: Visible above leafless treetops is what appears to be a black ring against a gray sky. That most likely would have been the end of the story, but newswires picked up the image, as did United Press International.

Earlier in the summer, two Springfield police officers out on patrol saw a weird object above the village of North Springfield. Intrigued, they followed it in their cruiser. Because the object was low and wasn't moving as fast as an airplane, they were able to keep relative track of it. That was, until they reached the junctions of Routes 10 and 103 in the adjacent town of Gassetts. As they watched, the object continued on its way, heading west, then disappearing from sight behind a hill.

Ultimately, no one can say what it was about Vermont in 1966 that warranted such activity. The *Times Argus* claims that reports from that period "have never been equaled in number or geographic scope."

It was all enough of an experience that local poet Pat Belding was moved to prose. The *Times Argus* published his poem, "Flying Saucer Questionnaire," on April 21, 1966:

Flying saucer blinking there / Are you swamp gas or a flare? / Are you fact or fabrication / Real or just hallucination? / Are you gathering dope on us / Using saucer scope on us / Filing data on our planet / As you hover low to scan it? / Were you born in outer space / Or is Earth your starting place? / We would really like to know — Are you friend or are you foe? / If you're cordial, come on down / Land your ship somewhere near town / Then why not drop in for tea. / U.F.O. — R.S.V.P.!

We should add that the offer still stands.

NO SLOWDOWN IN ACTIVITY
Despite the fact that these days, with so many of us taking the default position of casting our eyes decidedly *downward*, transfixed on our electronic devices, reports of unexplained phenomena continue to be plentiful. Entries in the National UFO Reporting Center (NUFORC) and the Mutual UFO Network (MUFON) databases describe encounters with oblong, disc-shaped, and arrow-shaped objects with brilliant circulating lights; spheres, orbs, and globes of every hue that dance or stand still; glowing triangles, cross-shaped formations, flying crescents; fireballs, pulsating lights.

Here are a few to ponder.

Along the highway between Waterbury and Stowe, November 5, 2009: A passenger in a car saw something "huge" moving through the clouds. It was round or oval, she recalled, and "the leading edge of the object was very prominent." It appeared to be huge and heavy, just above the thin layer of clouds, and seemed to actually be "pushing the clouds along," according to the witness. Self-described as a former ranch owner accustomed to being outdoors and observing the sky, the viewer emphasized that it could not have been a flock of birds because they make arrows or straight lines—not round formations. Although it moved out of sight rather quickly, she was able to snap a photo. Taken through the car window, it captures a wide view of high clouds above a mountain ridge and treetops. Roughly at center, a vague half-circle shape seems to be outlined against the mottled sky.

In Springfield, November 16, 2012: A viewer sitting outside to catch some of the Leonid meteor shower suddenly noticed what he first identified as a "blinking star." It was very bright and alternated between red and blue. "Then I noticed that it was moving all over the sky; right, left, up, down," the witness recalled, adding that it occasionally stopped and hovered. It was spear-shaped, with the light emanating from its center and seeming to connect to its outer rim via long shafts of light. "It looked like some sort of craft, honestly," the observer added. "I don't know how to describe it."

In Waterbury, August 18, 2014: A self-described "fabricator and performance mechanic by trade" was sitting out on his front porch when a "huge caravan" of local, state, military, and unmarked vehicles barreled by. A helicopter soon followed. "This kind of thing never happens here," the witness wrote, "so I knew something big was going on."

He quickly discovered that they were responding to a call about a man babbling incoherently and threatening to harm himself.

The witness continued to watch the helicopters, claiming to see five or six in a span of five hours, circling a wider and wider area and spotlighting the woods. Coincidence or not, it was when the last chopper finally left the area that he sighted "the impossible."

It was 9:56—"I'll never forget that time."

A ball or orb of brilliant blue-and-white light, very much the same color as the "arc from a plasma cutter or torch" was sitting low in the trees. Its edges were particularly intensely lit. Quickly, it gained elevation until it was fully visible above the tallest spruce trees and then climbed an additional 500 feet. At that point, the witness described it making a series of seemingly random movements—first hovering, then moving due east, then "frantically and instantly" changing direction and speed. He compared the spectacle to the movements of a potentiometer, a mechanical arm that traces pen on paper.

Then it took what seemed to be an "interplanetary trajectory, or an interstellar one," progressively getting smaller, gaining speed, and finally disappearing from view. It left behind what the witness described as an "ominous feel" in the air. When he drove out to the field where he perceived its initial landing took place, he saw a vapor hovering a foot or two above the ground (but not occurring elsewhere).

"I still to this day have trouble contemplating the physics of what I saw. It made absolutely no sense," he wrote, adding, "I've seen shooting stars, I've seen supersonic jets break the sound barrier, I've seen space shuttles in orbit, I've seen the International Space Station float on by, I've seen meteors and meteorites, I've flown drones and seen military drones flown. This was none of the above."

In any case, he concluded, whatever it was, "It certainly was one hell of a spectacle."

———

In Newport, September 6, 2014: A couple enjoying a backyard bonfire spotted three "glowing red objects" flying low in a north-northeast trajectory, spaced about a minute apart from each other. At a certain point, each abruptly turned 90 degrees east, heading toward Montpelier. They made no sound and had no flashing lights as required by the FAA, and one witness estimated their speed at 400 miles an hour. He called a neighbor—who also witnessed it, along with his wife and daughter—and used an iPhone to take a photo. The image depicts a bright orange dot at about a 70-degree angle from the moon. At the bottom edge of the frame, a house with lit windows can be seen. "It was very odd," the witness wrote, describing the night as clear, 63 degrees, with a full moon. "It was way bigger and faster than commercial aircraft we see and hear all the time."

———

In Fairfax, December 4, 2014 (MUFON "Case 61834"): A witness working out in his basement suddenly saw an unusual bright light through the window; he quickly ran outside to get a better look.

"Before noticing any detail, I felt an intense sense of dread," he told MUFON researchers. "What I saw shocked me down to my core."

Perhaps a half-mile from where he stood, he saw an "extremely bright object, pulsating red and blue lights, bouncing around slightly." Describing himself as "transfixed but also fearful," he was able to pull himself away from the sight, run inside, and tell his wife. He also retrieved a travel telescope. As the husband related later, his wife "leaned toward the window, squinted her eyes, and her mouth dropped open."

Together they watched the disc-shaped object, whose pulsating lights appeared to come from inside, "passing out through its walls." A cylindrical, orange-yellow light illuminated the ground—a vacant cow pasture—directly below the strange craft. It seemed to home in on an unidentifiable angular white object. Looking through the scope, his wife then pointed out another visible body, what the witness described as "mostly black and camouflaged," and perhaps 200 or 300 yards closer. It slowly rocked "around and up and down," and he was eventually able to make out the rough outline of an enormous triangle.

The couple kept tabs on the objects throughout the night. Over time, the pulsating disc grew "calmer, more stationary, and less bright," its red light disappearing as the craft "appeared to settle into a lower-energy state." Eventually the disc and the triangle changed positions—the disc now higher—and he was suddenly able to see the full form of the triangle, hovering with its underside pointing directly toward his window and a faint, circular orange light at each of its three corners.

The following day, he recalled, he talked with a neighbor who corroborated his sighting. Suspecting the objects might return, he spent the next night with his eyes on the skies. And indeed, two bright, pulsating shapes appeared shortly before midnight, about a half-mile farther away.

"I watched for over an hour as they appeared to follow a grid pattern slightly above the treetops near a river," he explained. He concluded that Vermont is a "hot spot" for such phenomena and that "many people have reported similar objects in my area; MANY more have likely seen them and remained silent."

In Barre, February 15, 2015: A witness was walking home around nightfall when he saw an "unusually bright" star far off in the distance. As he focused his attention, it immediately began to move across the sky directly toward him—first at a "moderate" speed, then much faster. It finally stopped about 300 feet away from where he stood. Sitting in the sky at about 500 feet elevation was a sphere-shaped object, roughly 120 feet in diameter and "clearly honeycombed with dimples like a golf ball." It was soundless, featured a bright white light with a "goldish fluctuating tint" to it, and "appeared to be observing me as I just remained calm and stared up at it. This lasted about 5 minutes." Then, at first slowly, it took off to the west, and the witness marveled at its "incredible navigational control" as it increased "to warp speed or Mach speed" and then moved completely out of sight.

The witness identified himself as a 58-year-old former member of the US Coast Guard who was trained as a navigation technician to search for lights during missions off the waters of Maine and Canada.

In Peacham, April 14, 2015: An observer sitting on a porch looking east noticed a stationary object with two lights of a "warm white/ soft bronze color." They remained illuminated for about three seconds and then were extinguished. About five seconds later, "three arrangements of light" appeared in roughly the same vicinity; two of the lights were lower than the third, which sat up and to the right of the others. These were also stationary. Again, within a matter of seconds, they, too, flickered out. "Several heartbeats later," a singular set of lights appeared in tandem with the formation of three lights.

As the observer continued to watch, lights appeared and burned out two more rotations, these times moving closer to the tree line. The witness noted that this was not the first time he had seen "interesting lights" in the sky—other occasions were in fall 2012 and fall 2013. The observer added that they were accompanied by a "very subtle audible low rumbling." "That the 'objects' appeared stationary has me wondering," he wrote.

In Northern Vermont (about 30 to 45 minutes from the Quebec border), July 25, 2016: Driving through the "pitch black mountains," a man traveling with his family saw what looked to be an approaching motorcycle headlight in his rearview mirror. "It grew larger and larger REAL fast," he wrote, so he changed lanes to get out of its way. But nothing passed his car, and when he looked back to the rearview, it was gone. Five minutes later, it was suddenly back again, "gaining on us, real fast." Then, just as suddenly, it vanished again. "No sound, no vehicle, nothing?" he wrote, adding that there are no turnoffs along that dark and deserted stretch of road.

On August 18, 2018, the driver again encountered these "ghost rider" headlights. This time it gave the impression of suddenly appearing about 250 feet back rather than showing up farther off in the distance and rapidly gaining on him. Again, nothing passed him, and "whatever it was just vanished . . . again." He called it "very eerie" but "very fascinating and spooky" all at once. "Beginning to wonder WHY this happens to us," he finished. "Not sure what it was, but you get a sensation and feeling when you know something is not right."

In Newbury, July 29 and August 11, 2018: Observers described a "large yellowish triangle" floating against the clear night sky. "Both times the object remained stationary during our 10 minute viewing," the viewer wrote. "No sound was detected."

PROJECT BLUE BOOK FILES

Of the 13,000-plus cases investigated by the federal government between 1947 and 1969 as part of its Project Blue Book program, just 20 originated in Vermont. Many of those were quickly ruled out by officials, determined to be sightings of military or civilian aircraft, planets, meteors, weather balloons—even tracer bullets.

The following are instances in which no conclusions could be reached on the basis of presented data or where cases were classified as resulting from "unknown" origins.

On April 24, 1952, in Bellevue Hill, crewmembers of a C-124 cargo aircraft spotted three strange objects in the sky. Circular and bluish in color, they materialized 20 degrees to the right of the cargo ship, disappeared, then reappeared 20 degrees left of course. They then "very rapidly" faded from sight. The observers described their "loose fingertip formation" and performance of "straight and level maneuvers" at high speeds. Identifying the trio of craft by name as "flying saucers," the observers emphasized that they were sighted at roughly 5:00 p.m. on a clear day with unlimited visibility. **Conclusion:** "Unknown."

On May 6 and May 13, 1956 in Waterville and Morrisville, four separate observers reported similar formations composed of between two and six objects moving across the evening sky. Unusual to Project Blue Book reports, their names are all included with their testimonies—typically, names and exact locations are blacked out throughout each report. (Whether this was deliberate or an oversight, we can't be sure.) The consensus, according to the investigator: "Four objects shaped like a star, size of star. Color yellow—a light on [each] object. No sound, no exhaust, object was traveling very fast and became very bright. Silver colored, 4–6' diameter."

A Mr. Standcliff, a 37-year-old farmer, was one of the first observers on the 6th. He saw just three of the objects moving about 70 to 75 degrees above the horizon. The northernmost of them was moving from west to east; the center object from north to south as it "appeared to rise"; and the easternmost moving "very slowly" from east to west. Watching them for about two hours through binoculars, he estimated that they were four feet in diameter and about as large as a basketball held at arm's length. Curiously, they also seemed to have what looked like a box or a gondola suspended beneath them. "They were illuminated like an automobile head-light about a mile away," Standcliff recalled. They "made no sound or left no trails" and "appeared transparent and had the outline similar to a bright star."

The same night, a Mr. Wiltshire, a 46-year-old lathe operator, witnessed four objects "fanned out across the sky from east to west," located about 20 degrees above the horizon. The easternmost object was the only one that moved—but as it did, it moved "very fast in an approximate easterly direction." A week later, on the 13th, Wiltshire again witnessed the strange display, this time comprising six objects. Two were directly overhead and appeared brighter than the other four, which were located roughly 35 degrees above the horizon. He described them as varying between the size of a dime and the size of a grapefruit. They seemed to remain suspended, and like Standcliff, this time he spotted a triangular shape with a small tail suspended beneath them. "All objects appeared solid and had distinct edges," he recalled. "The smaller objects appeared as a bright star but retained a clear outline."

Also on the 13th, 36-year-old Robert H. Whitemore, a manager at First National Store, saw two of these (presumably) same objects, watching them for about an hour. "The object at the end of the sighting appeared to burst and disappear from view," he claimed. They were both "clearly outlined against the sky and were approximately the size of the bright stars."

What exactly they were may have been surmised by Fred Green. The 38-year-old manager of the Morrisville Foundry observed the four objects through 4X binoculars and said they appeared to be balloons attached to a gondola. About four to six feet in diameter, they were "silver colored as if made of aluminum or painted silver." He watched them for about two hours, and they made "no erratic movements."

The investigator reported that he called the Burlington Airport control tower but received a "negative report on any aircraft in the area." A call to the Burlington weather station also yielded null results—they said there had been no balloon releases either night. Similarly, a check with the 764th Air Force aircraft control and warning squadron based in Saint Albans revealed that there were several projects being conducted involving the use of balloons—but track logs showed no entries made on the dates of the sightings. Based on its relative shape and speed, he added, it could possibly have been a cluster of weather balloons with telemetering instruments attached.

Conclusion: "Possibly balloon."

On September 20, 1959 in Rutland, a housewife spotted a large, round, silver object making small circles in the sky as it traveled from east to west. "It proceeded in a generally straight path across the sky, except that it appeared to be turning or rotating in small arcs throughout the course of travel," according to the investigator. He added that the Rutland area is not within a controlled air space, the Bangor Air Defense sector was not controlling any interceptor aircraft at the time, and there was no known instrument flight rules (IFR) or visual flight rules (VFR) traffic.

Conclusion: "Insufficient data for evaluation."

On February 27, 1960, in Cornwall, "many witnesses," both civilian and military, saw something unusual moving along the sky on an eastern course. As succinctly summarized by the investigator, "Round object with appearance of a star like silver or reflected light, reddish in color at the head and fading to pale yellow toward the end. Object appeared to be descending. Object had tail that covered a 5–7 degree arc." The investigator notes that the "description and duration" seems to fit that of a jet aircraft with an afterburner in operation; indeed, a fighter group is stationed in the area where the sighting occurred. "It is possible that the witness[es] observed an aircraft through the inversion layer, with the illusion distorted to refraction."

Conclusion: "Reflection." "Possibly aircraft."

On August 4, 1960, in Clover, observers spotted what they said looked like a "a potbellied iron bar without wings" on a northern course. Appearing for a few seconds, it looked "red hot" and was "wide in the middle and flared into two long prongs at the tail." It pointed gradually downward, then disappeared behind the tree line.

Conclusion: "The description is not generally like a meteor; however, the duration and movement, as well as being red-hot, indicate this possibility. This report is correlated with one from Dexter, Maine."

On September 10, 1961, the North Concord Air Force Station reported something on their high-frequency radar that appeared to be the size of an aircraft—but it was flying at 62,000 feet (airplanes top out at about 35,000 feet) and moving far slower than a typical aircraft. It remained on the radar for roughly 18 minutes, moving gradually northwest to south. It first appeared at 196 degrees moving 84 miles an hour, then moved out of contact while at 199 degrees and traveling at 80 miles an hour. The investigator pointed out that its "relative low speed and high altitude, coupled with its erratic course, including hovering, indicate target was probably high-flying weather balloon."

Conclusion: "Probably balloon."

On July 29, 1967, in Brendon, a pair of witnesses reported "two glowing things" moving along the horizon. They were stargazing from Brandon Cemetery along US Highway 7 when they spotted the two lights, which moved slowly across the sky at about a 15-degree angle from the earth. The distance between the lights "never varied"—nor did the light they emitted, which was a "dull glow, pure white," according to the male observer. "The lights appeared to be either small and very close, or very large and far away." There was "completely silence in the air as well as the cemetery"; no engine noises could be heard. Therefore, the witness surmised, "It was definitely not a helicopter; no helicopter I know of has such a glide ratio without power." He also ruled out meteors because the lights were "equal in luminous intensity. It would seem to me that two meteors would not behave in such a manner." As for the possibility of a satellite? "Its position in the sky was inconceivable for that," the observer stated adamantly.

Conclusion: "Insufficient data for evaluation."

On November 27, 1968, in Brattleboro, an individual filed a report stating that he had seen UFOs on several occasions. In the most recent encounter, the witness recalled driving to the First National Shopping Center at around 5:00 p.m.; a large, white craft suddenly appeared and "hung in the sky like a star." "Great shafts of white light shot into the sky lighting up that area," the observer claimed.

In another example, the observer saw a large UFO with a white light at center, blue lights on top, and red lights on the bottom; on a third occasion, a saucer-shaped ship with a circle of revolving lights moved slowly from the north along the western horizon and then turned and moved south.

The witness added that strange craft can be seen on "any clear night" from his house, which commands a wide view of the sky to the west over a low mountain range. "They appear in such number and so frequently [that] anyone can see them." Notably, their shared characteristics are that they "keep low. They fly up and down and sideways. They make no sound."

Furthermore, the observer adds, "during the last six months the UFOs have become much more numerous and are now of a more sophisticated design. We feel that we are under constant surveillance. Twice I'm sure a small red one followed me."

The purported frequent observer also provided a possible answer as to why the Green Mountain State had such a frequency of reported activity. "Apparently they congregate here in southern Vermont because the mountains keep our radar from finding them." **Conclusion:** "Unreliable report."

Perhaps the observer is correct—but that doesn't inhibit them from continuing to find us . . .

FIVE
CONNECTICUT
A Case for Everything

I want to stand as close to the edge as I can without going over. Out on the edge you see all the kinds of things you can't see from the center.

—KURT VONNEGUT

ALL OF A SUDDEN, HE WAS BATHED IN LIGHT. AS IT WAS DUSK AND he was walking along a residential road near his home, his initial instinct was to step out of the way of an oncoming car. But then he saw huge, edgeless shadows on the ground; also, why didn't he hear an approaching motor or the crunching of wheels on gravel?

He looked up—and that's when he saw a huge ball of light. A few hundred feet above him, moving at tremendous speed. In the second he had to assess whatever it was, he caught what he later described as a sphere, fiery bright, making no sound, leaving no trail.

This report comes from Wauregan in the northwest, or "quiet corner," of Connecticut; it was one in a series of sightings investigated by the US government in March 1954.

Although small, Connecticut—take your pick of nicknames: the Nutmeg State, the Constitution State, the Provision State—is indefatigable when it comes to UFO activity.

It was, in fact, the location of one of the earliest UFO sightings, as inscribed for all history by Reverend Cotton Mather. Centuries later, more than 60 cases from Connecticut were taken up in the 1940s, 1950s, and 1960s during the government's Project Blue Book, and there are upwards of 1,500 entries (continuing to the present day) in the National UFO Reporting Center's online database. Not to mention hundreds of other supposed encounters, run-ins, and "abductions" that are documented on numerous other witness reporting websites, including the Mutual UFO Network (MUFON).

The so-called Hudson Valley UFO is said to have taken a few diverting passes over Connecticut, and locals have reported and purportedly experienced just about every encounter imaginable (and, sometimes, imagined). Its skies cloak many secrets that beg to be explored.

MATHER SHIP . . . OR *MOTHER* SHIP?

Actually, the Reverend Cotton Mather wasn't the one who did the sighting, but he did record it for history's sake.

The Puritan minister, British government ouster, and prolific author—his writings on witchcraft, in fact, helped feed the hysteria that culminated in the travesty of the Salem Witch Trials—wrote in his *Magnalia Christi Americana* of an account he received from a pastor in New Haven.

In 1648, James Pierpont described an ethereal ship that appeared in the air above the city's harbor following a great thunderstorm. When the hemisphere had returned "serene" about an hour before sunset, this ghost of a vessel floated aloft "seemingly with her sails filled under a fresh gale, holding her course north, and continuing under observation, sailing against the wind, for the space of half an hour."

Many were drawn to "behold this great work of God," Pierpont relayed, with children crying out, "There's a brave ship!" In his poetic terms, the Connecticut reverend described the craft as "crouding [*sic*] up as far as there is usually water sufficient for such a vessel" and near enough to spectators that they could throw a stone onboard her (if she had a material form).

But quickly enough, her main-top was blown off, followed by her masts, and "after the hulk brought unto a careen, she overset, and so vanished into a smoaky [*sic*] cloud." These billows and mists quickly dissipated, leaving, "as everywhere else, a clear air," Pierpont wrote.

He explained what he (and the rest of New Haven) considered to be her cause: A year earlier, in January 1647, several passengers boarded a 150-ton ship and sailed off with the bad omen that "she would prove their grave." A Reverend Davenport accompanied and attempted to appease them, however, offering the words "Lord, if it be thy pleasure to bury these our friends in the bottom of the sea, they are thine; save them!"

Whether by jinx or coincidence, the ship never returned, and "New Haven's heart began to fail her." "This put the Godly people on much prayer, both publick [*sic*] and private, that the Lord would (if it was his pleasure) let them hear what he had done with their dear friends."

When the ghost ship appeared, onlookers overcome with emotion noted its marked resemblance to the long-lost ship, including its coloring, rigging, and proportions. "This was the mould [*sic*] of their ship, and thus was her tragick [*sic*] end," the reverend wrote.

Still, it was not a sad tiding—or vision. It was, in fact, a confirmation and a reassurance.

For "God had condescended, for the quieting of their afflicted spirits, this extraordinary account of his sovereign disposal of those for whom so many fervent prayers made continually."

BUT FIRST, ONE POSSIBLE EXPLANATION?

It appeared in a 1950 *New York Times* story along with the blaring headline "COULD THIS BE ONE?" Spherical, wingless, and almost cartoonishly yellow, the Vought V-173 is one possible culprit for the rash of UFO sightings—not to mention conspiracy theories that the US government was developing its own flying saucers—in postwar America.

Conceived by aeronautical engineer Charles Zimmerman in the 1930s, the V-173 was a wingless or "all wing" experimental fighter plane developed for the US Navy during World War II. It was known for its hovering ability, its maneuverability at low speeds, and for being almost impossible to stall. Described as a "flying pancake," its shape allowed for near-vertical takeoff and landing (particularly useful for operation from US Navy ships).

So, *literally*, this thing was a flying saucer. No surprise that it could be mistaken for something out of this world.

According to *Connecticut Magazine*, it won a design contest put on by the National Advisory Committee for Aeronautics (NACA), the precursor to NASA. Yet, impressed as they were, the government organization declined to develop it because it was "too advanced." So the enterprising Zimmerman brought it to the Vought-Sikorsky Aircraft Plant in Stratford (in Fairfield County on Long Island Sound), which built its prototype. Boone T. Guyton piloted its maiden flight, out of Bridgeport Municipal Airport—now Igor I. Sikorsky Memorial Airport—on November 23, 1942. After some experimenting with taxiing and hops, Guyton flew it for 13 minutes, reaching 100 miles an hour.

Test flights continued. As the story goes, Charles Lindbergh, a onetime consultant for Vought, became an advocate for the unique craft after Guyton flipped it on the beach—both he and the craft both coming out unscathed. Lindbergh apparently even flew it on several occasions.

Eventually, more advanced prototypes were ordered and built, including the XF5U-1, with a 16,000-horsepower radial engine and the capability for 425-mile-per-hour speeds. But development lagged as Vought focused on other planes, then jets, following World War II.

Eventually, the plans were abandoned altogether. Still, the craft exists, part of the extensive collection of the Smithsonian Institution.

Alas, Zimmerman's concept never went into mass production, and it remains just a footnote—or perhaps "asterisk" would be more accurate—in the history of aviation. Not to mention an enigma for many a star-gazer.

MEANWHILE, BACK TO 1954 . . .

. . . and that beam of light and racing ball in the sky. Mr. Anonymous (as we'll call him; his name is blacked out in the Project Blue Book report) was walking through his neighborhood in Wauregan— located in the state's northwest, or "quiet corner"—at the time of his encounter. He told an investigator (whose name is also scrubbed from the documents) that it was headed "due north . . . directly toward the North Star." He was "positive" that the object was not a plane, "not only because of lack of sound, but because of extreme speed." The investigator adds that Mr. Anonymous is a man that he knows well "and whose veracity I would never question."

An almost identical report came from eight miles away; an observer speaking emphatically in Polish (as translated by his daughter-in-law) described being suddenly enshrouded in a bright white light. When he looked up, he saw a flaming object about 200 feet in the air, heading north.

The bright ball of light was similar to one seen over Danielson, Plainfield, Moosup, Jewett City, Norwich, and New London to the southeast of the state, causing "enough consternation" that local newspaper the *Norwich Bulletin* and the police barracks were "besieged" with telephone calls. Among the witnesses, the investigator underscores, was a group of men in Norwich that included pilots, former pilots, and engineers. They saw the object through "powerful glasses" and surmised that it had its own source of energy because of the manner of its movements. One man of this group, in fact, professed that it caused "strange and unusual disturbances" in this television set.

Although at separate sides of the state, the incidents were investigated in tandem.

The consensus: The object was elliptical, about the size of an orange when seen with the naked eye, and exceptionally bright—so much so that observers "felt the necessity of shielding their eyes." It was metallic but changed colors, and its top portion seemed to glow orange and red (almost as if it was on fire or engulfed in flames). Two observers said it looked hollow in its center, while others described "some sort of tail assembly." It vacillated movements between horizontal and vertical, slow and swift, and appeared in a space far above typical flight paths. At all times, it was soundless.

Although the official conclusion is that it was most likely an upper-air research balloon or a meteor, the investigator seems to have doubts. "All observers agree that object was something like which they'd never witnessed before," he reports, noting that it was unlikely to be a jet because of the lack of sound and that it being a comet was "doubtful" because of its flat trajectory and no discernible tail. "As to its being a fireball, I do not know. Because of soundlessness, that fact might be doubtful also."

Most interesting of all? It was seen in at least two places at the same time. That's "a real indication of the thing's speed," the investigator concludes.

But an otherworldly speed? We can never know for sure.

LITTLE GREEN MEN? NOT THESE GUYS

At first, Mary M. Starr legitimately thought there was a "crippled airplane" in her backyard.

Starr (the name is quite fitting, no?) was alone in her Old Saybrook home on December 16, 1957; around 2:00 a.m., she was abruptly awakened by a harsh light and, creeping to the window to check it out, saw what looked to be a small craft in her back garden. Brightly lit, it seemed to be the shape and size of a small prop plane. Had there been some sort of crash?

But "when I got my eyes really open" and shook the sleep off, she recalled, she saw that the object was actually *hovering* just above her clothesline between the house and the garden shed. All told, it was about 20 to 30 feet long, dark gray, cigar-shaped, with no wings, fins, or other appendages. Most remarkably, though, were its portholes—well, not the portholes themselves, exactly, but what she was able to see through them.

Inside the craft, she was confounded to see three "beings" bustling about with their arms raised. Their anatomy was peculiar and unlike anything she'd ever come across: There were no visible hands, and their heads were square or rectangular, red-orange in color with a brighter red "bulb" at their center (she later said that this could have been her interpretation of helmets they wore). Their clothing: jackets that "flared out" at their base.

Because the craft was so shallow, these creatures could not have been more than three and a half or four feet tall, she said.

She saw nothing else discernible inside the object before the porthole lights suddenly faded. It was then that the shell of the craft began glowing brightly, and a six-inch antenna arose, "oscillating and sparkling." It soon retracted, and the strange object began to move, making a sharp right-angle turn before gliding smoothly above the ground, dipping and undulating with the earth's contours. Then it tilted sharply, shot up in the sky at "terrific speed" and in total silence—and totally disappeared.

As most of the homes in her neighborhood were unoccupied that time of year (it being a beach town), Starr was the sole witness to the bizarre encounter. Notifying authorities, she was later questioned by Richard Hall and Isabel Davis of the National Investigations Committee on Aerial Phenomena (a research group based in Washington, DC, that was in active operation from the 1950s to 1980). They identified Starr as a former teacher holding a master's degree from Yale, who seemed credible and of sound mind.

"Because of her background, and because she had no conceivable reason to invent or embellish such a story," neither investigator could find any reason to "dismiss her report out of hand," they concluded.

Still, Starr's detailed experience, like hundreds of others chronicled in voluminous reports, leaves an indelible question mark.

"NOT CONVINCED" BY FINDINGS

The official conclusion was that it was an astronomical phenomenon—a particularly spectacular view of Venus—but Alice Danuszar was having none of it. The 49-year-old Sandy Hook resident stood firm in her conviction and the facts she reported on February 22 and 23, 1966.

"At first I thought I was seeing things, but I know what I saw," she told the local newspaper (whose name is not included in the extensive report).

And that was? A funnel-shaped object brighter than a star; blue-green and metallic; moving up, down, and sideways in the sky at daybreak. She spotted the object two days in a row; it appeared just before sunrise in the eastern sky and slowly moved southwest.

The object was shaped "somewhat like a TV tube with the base end downward or somewhat like an ice-cream cone," she recalled. "A metallic bluish-green flame came from the bottom, and at various intervals red antennae appeared to thrust upward from around the top in different numbers at a given moment."

Those ranged from two to five in various combinations, she said. Meanwhile, "It did not stay in one spot but appeared to hover, then go to one side and another and up and down, changing position from time to time."

Although she described herself as "scared," she watched the object through binoculars for at least an hour, then said she finally dared to call her brother at 4:55 a.m. One Conrad Fleischmann, as well as her neighbors Mr. and Mrs. Phillip Britton, "thought I was crazy" at first, she acknowledged. But then they viewed the object and corroborated her story, saying it definitely wasn't a helicopter and didn't at all resemble an airplane.

Danuszar was so resolute in what she saw that she contacted local authorities, eventually filling out a seven-page "US Air Force Technical Information" questionnaire, complete with diagrams and several Q&A sections. In that document, she also included a rough drawing of what looks like a funnel.

The official conclusion? It was a particularly bright Venus sighting. Another possibility: The Robert Fulton Company in nearby Danbury had announced its testing of a rescue balloon.

"I think I should know a balloon when I see one," Danuszar scoffed. "I'm not a saucer watcher. I just stumbled on it by chance." She added, "I can't afford to make a darned fool of myself. I know I'm not nuts or anything."

The newspaper reported that other residents of Sandy Hook had also recently seen "strange saucers" and other objects in the sky, and they shared her sentiments. They wanted to know what it really was. "Is it Earth made, or has it come from outer space?" they asked.

Which is, after all, the enduring question for all of us.

THE "HUDSON VALLEY UFO"? BUT THIS IS CONNECTICUT

In the 1980s there were mass sightings—in the thousands—of a flying object widely described as boomerang- or "V"-shaped with multicolored lights. With no apparent explanation for its origin or presence, this came to be known by ufologists and other trackers and enthusiasts as the "Hudson Valley UFO." Whatever it was, though, its path apparently strayed a little north, as well.

Between 1982 and 1987, the strange craft was seen as far east as New Haven (on Long Island Sound) and as far north as Brookfield (inland, in the middle of the state). One witness, identified as an executive with IBM, spotted it along the Interstate 84 corridor in 1983; he described it as bigger than a 747 and hanging in the air like it was on a string. Another man, Arnold Springster, provided in-depth detail to author Philip Imbrogno: Appearing about 200 feet over his car, it was "dead quiet," "so huge" (easily the size of a football field) that it took a long time to pass over, made up of dark gray material with "low reflectability" that appeared smooth and "soldered together" and had a series of red and white lights. His description of its shape matched the boomerang or half-circle identified by many others, and he suggested that "I knew no aircraft could possibly keep that altitude and go so slow."

May 26, 1987, in particular yielded a cluster of viewings. Between 9:30 and 10:15 p.m., more than 200 people across New Milford, Southbury, and Newtown phoned police about a UFO. Several drivers pulled over to view it as it passed over Interstate 84; some even claimed that their cars lost power as it passed. Among these witnesses was Randy Etting, a commercial airline pilot on a nighttime walk in Newtown. Scanning the skies—as he often did, given his profession—he noticed unusual orange and red lights coming out of the west. Getting a closer look with binoculars, he saw a semicircular pattern of bright, multicolored lights, which seemed to be connected to an object that was larger than a football field.

At least one official explanation was bounced to the public: It was a formation of ultralight aircraft, painted black with colored lanterns, flying out of a local airport. Most people weren't convinced, however, and the case remains one of the most enigmatic in UFO history.

MAYBE THEY JUST WANTED TO FISH, TOO?

It plummeted out of the sky at around 2:00 a.m.—green, glowing, as big as a whale. As most of the area was swathed in sleep, it splashed into Bantam Lake in Litchfield, presumably sinking to the bottom of Connecticut's largest natural lake. But at least two people served as witnesses to the bizarre event on April 10, 2012: one, an unidentified motorist who phoned 911; the other an on-duty state police trooper about 10 miles away in Warren. The latter radioed in to Troop L barracks in Litchfield, reporting a large object falling from the sky; this triggered dispatch to send firefighters from the towns of Morris and Bantam, according to the *Litchfield County Times*, which made several passes up and down the lake in a boat—without result.

Quickly, the story was picked up by the Associated Press and went international, with many a joke made about radioactive whales and water-pruned gray bodies washing ashore and local businesses offering "stellar rates" and "Aliens Welcome" signs. There were also some reports of an unusual amount of dead fish washing up, but officials with the state Department of Energy and Environmental Protection said this had been occurring weeks earlier—a phenomenon caused by warm weather depleting water oxygen levels.

Ultimately, the official consensus was that it was a meteorite, and although there was initial hubbub, there's been little follow-up since. As state legislator Andrew Roraback put it to the *Times*, "We have added this to the list of life's unanswered questions."

PROJECT BLUE BOOK FILES

Among the 60-plus cases that were investigated by the government over a near 20-year period, those included here are instances where conclusions were "possible" (even dubious), not stated, unknown, inconclusive, or other.

In the "other" category, one of the most compelling involves a "Mrs. Cook" on the occasions of January 22 and January 29, 1952, in the Norwalk area. While driving to the store on a "lovely crisp night" on an empty road, the mother to a five-year-old daughter and a two-year-old son employed at the Remington Rand factory spotted white lights "emitting great brilliance" at about 10 o'clock on her car windshield. They were approaching from the east from a far point on the horizon, and they were "big—terribly big" and "like searchlights, only there was no diffusion."

The lights flew straight west and then changed direction and turned south, hanging in the air over the Armory Building at the intersection of Connecticut and Stevens Avenues. She was "amazed at the rapidity of its motion," she told investigators. The witness further described the object as dome-shaped, perfectly smooth, flat on the bottom, "perfectly rounded" at the top, 80 or 90 feet wide, the color of dull stainless steel, and about the height of a two-story home. "It's the most beautiful piece of mechanism I have ever seen—it's out of this world," she marveled. "I would not call it a flying saucer—I would call it a ship."

Her report goes into even more detail; as she watched for five or six minutes while stopped in the middle of the road, she could see a vast amount of machinery inside the craft, which also emitted a "beautiful" indirect and soft white light. Calling it a "work of art," she described a surface covered with patterns of lines "too highly intricate to accurately describe" that were angular, differently shaped, yet all the same size and evenly spaced. Furthermore, there were no bolts, joints, doors, or landing gear.

She estimated that about six men could walk shoulder to shoulder around the ship. And although she saw nothing, she described a distinct feeling of being watched. Still, she said, she had a "peculiar sensation of no fear."

After hanging motionless in midair for several minutes, the craft traveled out of sight over a hill, making no sound and leaving behind no vapor trail.

One week later, on January 29, Mrs. Cook professed to seeing the same "thing" again from the window of the Remington Rand restroom. This time, it appeared to be the size of a nickel and traveled at a "terrific rate of speed."

The wife and mother interviewed with US Air Force personnel, filled out extensive reports and paperwork, and drew diagrams of what she had seen. Investigators also probed her background, discovering she had had a brain tumor as a child that was removed, and schooling—she attended but didn't finish business college and art school. They also interviewed one of her bosses at Remington Rand, where she worked assembling electrical and mechanical devices. The assistant personnel manager said the witness vacillated in temperament between a "very pleasant girl, good worker, intelligent" to "loud, belligerent, and flying off the handle" when provoked.

Mrs. Cook, for her part, said she was familiar with the silhouettes of "helicopters, dirigibles, seaplanes, transports, fighters, and flying advertisements" and was "quite able to distinguish one from the other." This craft, though, was entirely different.

Ultimately, officials came to the conclusion that the source was "psychological," noting that the source is considered by some to be "a bit neurotic," the description bordered on fantasy, and the general impression is that the experience was "a figment of the observer's imagination."

Is it? Or is that just what they would like us to think?

DEEPER IN THE FILES

On March 10, 1950, in Bethel, a witness saw what he deemed "The Wing Saucer from Outer Space." Emitting a brilliant white light and flying 8,000 feet up, it was jet black and looked to have an enclosure of transparent glass. Making no sound, it circled overhead four times and then banked left at 25 degrees. When tilted, a white light was visible at the bottom of its wings. It was in sight for three minutes and then revolved at a slow rate of speed and disappeared northeast. The witness proclaimed, "This is a true report of what I have seen in the sky . . . so help me God." **Conclusion:** "Psychological." Investigators called it "highly improbable" that four naval aircraft in the same area on a clear day did not report any unusual craft.

On October 10, 1950, in New Haven, observers saw an object summarized in a report as "Starlike object 10 times brighter than VENUS. Steady orange glowing color. Steady light, not blinking. No sound, trail, or exhaust observed." It moved at a west-to-south course toward New York City at an estimated altitude of at least 20,000 feet and a speed between 400 and 700 miles per hour, according to the viewer. It was in sight for about 20 seconds and then "turned before disappearing."
Conclusion: "Aircraft (Possible)."

On December 27, 1953, in Madison, observers sighted what they described as "definitely a large ball of light. Slightly greenish." It was moving west, parallel to the earth, and observed at an angle of roughly 30 degrees. There was a "possible" slight humming noise, and the craft was "TREMENDOUS." It hung around for about 30 seconds, suddenly stopped, then slowly faded away.
Conclusion: "Possibly a jet aircraft which performed a 90 degree turn and flew directly away from observer."

On May 10, 1955, in Terryville, a witness described an object that was the size of a pea held at arm's length. It was observed for about a minute. "Sounded like an aircraft. Moving very fast. Object was at first blue in color but disappeared as though it had burned itself out."
Conclusion: "Possible jet aircraft with after burner."

On July 30, 1955, in Winsted, a round, silver object, the size of a baseball at arm's length, was seen flying northwest to northeast. It was in view for roughly five minutes.

Conclusion: "It is possible that the observer saw an aircraft passing to the north, and the sun being directly behind, he possibly saw the reflection off a passing aircraft."

On August 30, 1955, in Old Greenwich, observers submitted a sighting accompanied by a 35-millimeter color film transparency. "I was sitting around talking with the family on the back porch and I just happened to look up and notice this very bright object moving across the sky," the witness, a self-described UFO enthusiast, describes in his report. It moved south-southwest to north-northeast "at what must have been a great speed because of the short time that it took to vanish." He estimated the object to be about 150 feet in diameter, disc-shaped, and constructed of light metal.

In the film, the object appears about the size of a pinhead and resembles a "blue-white elliptical object with a trail." According to the report, it was examined by six separate photo specialists and Air Force scientists, at micro- and macroscopic levels with color and black-and-white prints of various densities. The consensus was that the object was caused by a flaw "either accidental or induced" in the film; that it could have been a small coating defect or a tiny particle of chemical substance clinging to the emulsion during processing, "causing a somewhat erratic reaction." Analysts also marveled that the object in question was "almost perfectly centered" in the film, "a remarkable feat" when dealing with such a small target so far away, "against a black backdrop, and through a viewfinder."

Conclusion: "(Other) Hoax."

On July 17, 1956, in Windham Center, a viewer identified as a "male student" saw "two objects like a star, the size of pea, color like a bright star, sound deep throbbing with vapor trails." Spotted a mile or more away in the southeast and then again in the northwest, the objects seemed to collide and then disappeared, with just one reappearing. A vapor trail appeared later on a night that was clear, dry, cool, with no wind. Traveling at an estimated 1,000 miles an hour, the supposed crafts "broke up and exploded." Until that point, the witness thought they were meteors.
Conclusion: "Imagination."

On July 28, 1956, in Meriden, a female witness reported a long, cigar-shaped craft with a bright glow. "Color white. Faded out." It was in view for 13 minutes in the southwest. The report states that the "chief observer" was a 40-year-old woman married to a crane operator and was "considered very reliable."
Conclusion: "Insufficient data for evaluation."

On August 25, 1956, in New Briton, a viewer offered this brief report: "One object round, size of quarter, color white, very bright—moved north directly away." It was observed for about two minutes.
Conclusion: "Insufficient data for evaluation."

On August 19, 1959, in Shelton, a "strange object" was reportedly seen by "six adults of average intelligence." As relayed by one of them in a letter, it was a little after 9:00 p.m. when the group saw something in the sky "moving rapidly" in a northeast direction.

After viewing it for about a minute, they concluded that it was not a shooting star or a jet—they thought maybe it was a satellite or a spent cone, "as it wobbled or spiraled at all times." Its brightness and color was that of a "first magnitude star," and as it passed overhead, it turned to an intense orange-red. The witnesses watched the object for about three minutes until it vanished. "Its altitude was hard to determine," the writer concludes, "but comparing to the stars, it seemed to be among them."

Conclusion: "Insufficient data for evaluation."

On March 14, 1960, in Waterbury, a viewer states very simply in a letter that "I observed what we believed was a flying saucer." (We being the observer and his/her mother, father, and sisters.) It moved slowly enough for them to watch it for a few minutes and was "flying at a high altitude, circular in shape, and very brightly lighted."

Conclusion: "No conclusion can be drawn on the information received."

On June 28, 1963, in North Branford, residents of rural neighborhoods on Circle Drive and Lea Drive spotted a basketball-sized bright white light. Its qualities, per the official report: "Erratic motion. Changed brightness. No trail. Disappeared behind clouds. Circular shape. Yellowish tinge. Speed estimated at 900 mph. Motion included reverse direction. No sound."

Observers watched it for three and a half minutes and guessed that it was about 500 feet up and traveling at a 45-degree angle. It seemed to be self-luminous, getting "real bright" at times with "beams coming out of it," and moved seamlessly—without turning—forward and backward.

Conclusion: "Insufficient data for evaluation." Seemingly perplexed investigators write, "It could have been a balloon, an aircraft, a star/planet."

On December 21, 1965, in Putnam, a pilot with (the now-defunct) Northeast Airlines out of Boston reported an unknown, quarter-sized, round object. Flying at 10,000 feet, he described the object as passing directly in front of his plane. "It was pink, then orange, then white," and after about seven minutes, it changed course, "picked up speed and disappeared." The report indicates that a US Navy aircraft was also in the area around the same time and did not sight or come into contact with the floating, colorful sphere. **Conclusion:** "No data to indicate object could NOT have been an A/C."

On September 17, 1967, in Taftville, three motorists stopped to get a better look at a large fluorescent light in the sky. It was sharp, solid, and "as large as the moon," heading northeast-east and shifting between a stationary position and slow movement. As it turned, observers caught sight of what they described as "two windows completely separated but very close to each other." (This they accompanied with a hand-drawn rendering of a circular object with two rough square/rectangular shapes at its center.) There was no noise at all, and suddenly the lights went out, and "the object was nowhere to be seen." The observer, identified as an eighth-grade student interested in UFOs, professing that, "as we live in a rural area, there were no other aircraft or lights around, so we could not be mistaken."
Conclusion: "Insufficient data for evaluation."

On Jan 12, 1968, in Westport, a pithy report states that an observer sighted numerous red and white blinking lights that seemed to rotate in a circular pattern. They watched the strange phenomenon—which was accompanied by no sound—for more than four minutes. **Conclusion:** "Possible (Aircraft)"

ADDITIONAL CASE FILES

At Hawthorne Beach Estate, 1932 or 1933: Two witnesses noticed a craft flying over Long Island Sound that was much faster than any they had seen before. As they watched, it made a sharp turn to the left into the rays of the setting sun, passing directly above them at great speed. They described it as cigar-shaped, "huge" compared to any other plane, with no rudder or wings. It emitted a pink glow at its front, a light swirl of gray smoke along its sides, and disappeared into the northwest.

In Oakville, 1966: "A UFO appeared out of nowhere, and just hovered motionless." It had a "dim glow, white and blue," and made no sound. The viewers' AM radio went to static as it passed, traveling northeast, and they reported the strange but distinct taste of battery acid. "Not a smell, but a taste," they emphasized.

In Southbury, 1972: A family of six described a "silent, huge" craft that hovered above them at about 300 feet. It was black, "the size of a zeppelin, cigar-shaped," with a light scouring the ground in a vacant cow field. Very slow and very quiet, it featured six lights that flashed before blinking out. The adults in the group attempted to explain it away as a hot air balloon.

In New Hartford, July 18, 1990: A 51-year-old art history professor spotted a silent, domed disc floating a few feet off the lawn in her backyard. It was about the size of a Volkswagen, she said, with red, yellow, and white perimeter lights that flashed sequentially. After hovering for a few moments, it rose at an angle, accelerating between two trees, and disappeared. Physical traces in the form of numerous clumps of ash-like material were left behind in a rough, 25-foot-diameter circle about 120 feet from the house. According to the National Investigations Committee on Aerial Phenomena (NICAP), these were analyzed and were "not consistent" with natural elements used in control samples.

In Bridgeport, 1990: Two brothers claimed to miss several hours of time when they spotted and decided to follow a "stingray-shape like object." It was near sunrise, and they were alerted to it by an unreal sound. It was dark and "about the size of two football fields put together," with square-shaped openings to either side. "I was more amazed than afraid," one of the brothers wrote. After the object hovered over a local funeral home, it shot off "at the blink of an eye," and the siblings attempted to follow it, ending up by Long Island Sound; they returned home several hours later—but were perplexed when they tried to explain away all the time that had passed.

In Harwinton, 1995 or 1996: A husband and wife were driving home from a fishing trip when something huge cast a shadow over the road around them. As they reported to MUFON, they looked up to see what they described as a football-field-sized, disc-shaped object. Its surface was a slightly metallic gray—"battleship gray silvery" or like spray paint—and had a band of several dark or black panels across its upper half. According to the husband, these looked like the "dark-smoked" windows on a skyscraper. There was no sound and no flame or smoke, and the trees were not affected by its passage. When it appeared, it was no more than 100 feet above the trees, and it flew across their field of view and then disappeared. According to the husband, it "felt like everything was in slow motion." They submitted a drawing of something that very much resembled a flying saucer of old, with a band of windows rimming its middle. The MUFON investigator described the couple as in their 30s—the husband, a self-employed carpenter; the wife, an emergency room nurse. "The witness seemed sincere, stressed desire for anonymity," the investigator wrote. "Husband owns business and would not want to be publicly connected with a UFO sighting."

In Litchfield, October 2006: A mother awoke at around 4:15 a.m. to machinelike noises and a rectangular blue light shining through her draped windows. The noise became deafening, hurting her ears; she covered them and "became discombobulated, confused." Suddenly a reddish-orange sphere appeared, and she described the sensation of "the cells in my body being jumbled up" and the emanating "feeling of evilness." But it stopped as soon as it started, and when she glanced at the clock, it still read 4:15.

In New Haven, August 2008: Five unusual lights were reported at Old Grove Park, moving around one another, "pretty close together," hovering over the area of Milford or Stratford on Long Island Sound. They were in view for about 45 minutes, constantly in motion, and made no sound.

In New Haven, September 2008: The same viewer as the previous entry was walking in the park around dusk when the lights appeared again (only this time there were four of them). They flickered and danced "around and under one another and disappeared and reappeared." Several people gathered, according to the writer, "to exchange ideas about what they could be, but no one really knows." The entry claims that the police department and Coast Guard were notified, as was local newspaper the *New Haven Register*.

In Chester, March 2009: A man sitting in his car saw a large, roundish, bright yellowish object approaching. When it stopped and hovered, he alerted his wife and landlord, who came out to look. "We all agreed that this object was extremely large, bright and stationary, at least four times, if not more, as large and as bright as the largest star in the sky," the man wrote. "I just find it extremely odd that an object could or would sit stationary in the sky for such a length of time." After about 30 minutes, it moved in a northwesterly direction and faded into the distance.

The landlord corroborates the story, describing the sky as somewhat cloudy, making it tough to see the stars. "This object, however, was so bright it almost hurt my eyes," he wrote, adding that it shimmered with a golden light. Reflecting on the incident later, he noted that planets do not shimmer; also, stars do not change their position in the sky like "this thing did."

In Madison, August 2010: While setting up a campsite at Hammonasset State Park, a family spotted a diamond-shaped object that "pulsated" red-orange as it moved across the sky to the northeast. It moved along steadily, paused, then rapidly ascended to the east at a high angle of ascent and disappeared. The adult male viewer described the skies as clear, with abundant stars and a waning gibbous moon providing "significant lighting, enough so that I would expect an exhaust/vapor trail to be visible." But there was none visible, he said, and there was no sound, either.

In Woodbury, July 2012: A viewer saw "two visible and unidentifiable lights" in the northwest region of the sky. The main one was a "red triangular/sphere shape" that hovered "unlike any identifiable aircraft I've ever seen." Sighted alongside it was a white orb of light. They appeared to be moving in tandem.

In Lisbon, October 2012: A glowing, bright orange orb was seen beside a newly planted, 15-foot tree. The orb floated about halfway between the ground and the tree's crown and "just hovered in the same spot for a while," according to the witness.

In Bristol, April 2014: Several witnesses described seeing a grouping of dozens of orange lights in the sky. They seemed to move in formation from west to east before disappearing. One spectator said that several people were pulled over to the side of the road to view them.

In New Britain, August 11, 2014: A group of witnesses near New Britain General Hospital captured a photo of a brightly pulsating craft. In the photo, the object is unmistakably angular, with different levels and circular sections, a bright orange bottom, and lines and dots illuminated white and red. According to the observer, it "turned itself on and off at will" and looked like a "clear tube" with lit posts and lights extending from its outer shell. "There were no clouds, and it was clear as day although it was evening," according to the witness. "It was large in shape, so I believe it was close [but] I don't know!"

In Milford, December 2016: A man alone on Christmas Eve described four objects in a diamond formation in the area of his backyard. They moved in a formation that was "clocklike," except that one of them seemed to be having difficulty maintaining altitude. It shifted from a "brilliant blue" to a blood red, dropping straight down out of formation, incrementally getting lower and lower. Each time it dropped, the other three craft brightened in intensity and the "distressed" craft rose weakly. Then a fifth object appeared, and the viewer felt "waves of gratitude" from the other orbs. Then, he says, he came to because he was cold, and realized that 11 hours had passed. The sun was out, and back inside, every TV in the house had been turned on. "Perhaps we are being told something," the witness wrote.

In Guilford, January 2017: A witness reports that there are "round shapes burned into the grass in a field near my house," adding that these are visible on Google Earth and "show up in every secluded field in town. There are hundreds of them."

——•——

In Sandy Hook, October 2018: A driver traveling along State Route 34 between the Stevenson Dam and Great Ring Road spotted a large object floating at a low altitude. Lined with white lights, which were steady and not flashing, "it was way too low and noiseless to be a 747 jet, and moving too slowly and silently," the observer recalls. It appeared to be like a giant rectangular or triangular floating platform and was just a couple hundred feet above the treetops. When he turned off on Great Ring Road to try and get a better look, it was gone. He notes that "there were plenty of planes in the sky at the same time—at normal altitudes though."

——•——

In Simsbury, October 2018: A viewer who describes herself as a stay-at-home mom who "has never paid much attention to UFOs" was reveling in some quiet time around 6:00 a.m. before her children were awake. All of a sudden, she noticed a bright light shining in through the windows and seeming to slowly move across the bathroom floor. This was highly unusual, she explains: "We live deep in the forest, far away from neighbors. Our house is located on eight acres of forested land, and the bathroom is on the second floor." (In other words, it couldn't be a passing car.)

When she looked outside, she was shocked to see a gigantic rectangular shape moving slowly just above the tree line. It was humming slightly, and she estimated it to be about the size of a 747 airplane and less than 50 feet from the house. The bottom was lined with six rows of alternating red and white lights, which were dim, like car headlights, but "clearly round shaped." Blocking out the night sky as it glided by for about "60 long seconds," it then slowly drifted out of her sightline over the trees. She sums up the encounter with, "I know it was much too large to be a drone of any type, and all other indications about its shape, sound, height, and movement prevent me from believing it was anything identifiable as man-made."

⁓

In Danbury, November 2018: A witness took pictures and video of a "very bright sphere" in the sky that "kept changing colors and disappearing every five seconds." Every time it disappeared? It took the form of an atom, she says. "The color change and disappearance were very fast."

What's next? Keep your eyes skyward!

Six

RHODE ISLAND
Small Wonders

Space . . . is big. Really big. You just won't believe how vastly, hugely, mindbogglingly big it is.

—Douglas Adams

It's a classic image, something you'd expect out of a production still from the likes of *Plan 9 from Outer Space*. A metallic, perfectly proportioned saucer, rounded protrusions at its top and bottom, hovers in the sky above a set of power lines.

To anyone with even the slightest sense of skepticism, it is a dubious image: too crisp, clear, and clichéd; in a sense, too good to be true. But at the time—and still today, for some devout believers—it was iconic and legendary: clear, substantiated, photographic proof of a flying saucer.

The image in question: A black-and-white still (part of a series of seven) captured by Rhode Islander Harold Trudel in 1967 in East Woonsocket.

The southeasternmost New England state, Rhode Island is perhaps best known for its palatial seaside mansions, such as the

Breakers, swanky Newport, and the like for the regatta types, and dramatic vistas, including Block Island. But at just 48 miles north to south and 37 miles east to west, it is the smallest state in the country. As such, it's no surprise that "Little Rhody" has the least reported activity when it comes to UFOs. Even so, the area the legendary John Updike described as the "mysterious crabbed state" indeed holds mysteries in its skies.

THE TRUDEL FILES

June 10, 1967: A clear and sunny day. Harold Trudel, a 29-year-old married man and father of three, was driving along West Wrentham Road in East Woonsocket, a city in northern Rhode Island. An avid UFO watcher, the young man decided to stop, retrieve his camera, and get out of his car to scope out some high-tension lines. According to a report filed by retired Air Force colonel Wendelle Stevens, he had seen unidentified objects on three other occasions but had not captured any images to speak of.

Whether by pure luck, sixth sense, or premonition, within minutes a high-domed, disc-shaped, metallic flying object came into view in the west. Camera in hand, crouching among the foliage, Trudel began to snap pictures as the craft crossed the sky above the power lines.

"The object maneuvered about in the area, flitting from point to point like a bee." As a result, the photographer changed position several times, "trying to stay hidden," Stevens wrote in his report. "He did not want any possible occupants of the craft, *if* occupied, to become aware of his presence."

The flying object remained in sight for about five minutes—then flashed off to the north.

All told, Trudel captured seven images. Not discernible in the photographs: an antenna protruding from the central lower portion of the object, which, Trudel later emphasized during questioning, did not come into any kind of contact with the power lines.

Marvelously enough, just six days later, the sky-watcher again spotted the same craft (or one very nearly like it) and snapped several more pictures.

Trudel's photos, although today admittedly hokey and (most undoubtedly) contrived, represent an era in American history when regular, everyday people began turning their eyes skyward and wondering just what could be out there.

THE LIFESTYLES (AND SUPPORT GROUPS) OF THE RICH AND FAMOUS

In a blue Victorian mansion once called "the most elegantly finished house ever built in Newport," there is a haven for "experiencers." (They don't like the stigmatizing term "abductees.") Once a year every summer, they gather to share their claimed run-ins with extraterrestrial entities, as well as thoughts, theories, and otherwise general gossip in a judgment-free zone.

Their host is sympathetic socialite Anne Ramsey Cuvelier. Her family home on Narragansett Bay, codesigned by an Emerson and purchased by her great-grandfather in 1895, welcomes members of this exclusive and private group—what Cuvelier calls "not a club anyone wants to belong to."

Cuvelier, described as "elegant and garrulous" in a 2013 feature in *Vanity Fair*, doesn't claim any abductions but recalls that her father, World War II hero Rear Adm. Donald James Ramsey, often mumbled about seeing strange flying craft that hovered and tore off at "unimaginable speed."

"I want to get information out so these people don't have to suffer," she told reporter Ralph Blumenthal. "Nobody believes you. You go through these frightening experiences, and then you go through the ridicule."

Among members who agreed to have their names used were Linda Cortile, known for her well-publicized abduction in Brooklyn in 1989; Kathleen Marden, niece of abductees Betty and Barney Hill; and Barbara Lamb, a studier of crop circles who claimed to once have had a run-in with a reptilian being inside her home.

Occasional reporters, medical professionals, scientists, astrophysicists, as well as ufologists and the otherwise UFO-inclined also have been welcomed.

But perhaps most famous (or infamous) among the group's champions was the late John Edward Mack. A psychiatrist at Harvard Medical School and a Pulitzer Prize–winning biographer, he risked his career by taking the audacious stance that those claiming to be abducted were in fact telling the truth—that is, they were not insane or deluded; something had really happened to them, something they truly believed. He regularly joined the group at the palatial Newport mansion until his sudden death in 2004.

Born of a long line of scholars and medical pioneers, Mack graduated cum laude from Harvard Medical School. He went on to found one of the country's first outpatient hospitals; launched the first psychiatry department at Cambridge Hospital; and wrote a bestselling psychological study about Lawrence of Arabia, *A Prince of Our Disorder: The Life of T. E. Lawrence*, for which he was awarded the Pulitzer Prize.

Over the years he began to study the idea of consciousness expansion—this as he traveled the world; prolifically wrote and studied; and gave lectures about numerous subjects, including the Arab–Israeli conflict—and came to be connected with Budd Hopkins. Considered the godfather of the alien abduction movement, Hopkins was a painter and sculptor who began studying the lives and experiences of abductees and authored several volumes, including the 1987 bestseller *Intruders: The Incredible Visitations at Copley Woods* (which also became a television miniseries).

After meeting Hopkins, Mack was fascinated by experiencers, and he began to theorize that beings didn't have to come from outer space, merely a parallel dimension. He wrote several books on his studies, including *Abduction: Human Encounters with Aliens* (1994) and *Passport to the Cosmos: Human Transformation and Alien Encounters* (1999).

"These individuals reported being taken against their wills, sometimes through the walls of their houses, and subjected to elaborate intrusive procedures which appeared to have a reproductive purpose," he wrote. "In a few cases they were actually observed by independent witnesses to be physically absent during the time of the abduction. These people suffered from no obvious psychiatric disorder, except the effects of traumatic experience, and were reporting with powerful emotion what to them were utterly real experiences. Furthermore, these experiences were sometimes associated with UFO sightings by friends, family members, or others in the community, including media reporters and journalists."

"In short," he concluded, "I was dealing with a phenomena that I felt could not be explained psychiatrically, yet was simply not possible within the framework of the western scientific worldview."

After an exposé by the *Boston Globe*—with the mocking headline "Aliens Land at Harvard!"—he appeared on the *Oprah Winfrey Show*. He declared to the eponymous host' "Every other culture in history . . . has believed there were other entities, other intelligences in the universe. Why are we so goofy about this? Why do we treat people like they're crazy, humiliate them, if they're experiencing some other intelligence?"

Still, his credibility was crimped, and Harvard did an inquest, accusing him of failing to do systematic evaluations to rule out psychiatric disorders and of pressuring patients to think they had been abducted. The prestigious school kept him on, but Mack remained notorious.

Until the end, though, he remained dedicated to what "abductions" and encounters could reveal about the cosmos, urging the scientific investigation of abductees—what he called a "science of human experience," stressing "the value of the authentic 'Witness.'"

"If what these abductees are saying is happening to them isn't happening," he would repeatedly ask, "what is?"

The question still lingers.

THE GOVERNMENT INVESTIGATES

Remarkably, over the entire 17-year period that the US government operated Project Blue Book—and detailed more than 13,000 sightings in hundreds of thousands of pages—there are just three formal reports from the Ocean State.

The first, from October 20, 1962, in seaside Bristol, describes "two 11-year-old youths [who] found objects that supposedly fell to earth with whooshing sound." The two elementary-schoolers informed their science teacher that they had been fishing on the Warren River when they suddenly witnessed a "gray object falling from the sky" that landed about 20 feet from them. The main "specimen" was described as a brown ball, three inches long, with a yellowish bubble suspended in middle of it that "looked like the yolk of a good-sized duck egg." When they found it, it was "warm" to the touch, but they said they were too afraid to pick it up. At the teacher's urgings, they brought the fragment to school, and it was turned over to authorities at the US naval base in Newport. Analysis found it to be polyethylene and plastic residue of type

66 nylon; the report describes it as "tailings" or "end-of-run" from extrusion machines that produce plastic forms or foils. Furthermore, "tests have indicated that none of the samples have been exposed to a space environment or have been used in relation with any space application."

But while there were plastic factories in Rhode Island at the time (and continue to be), none were located that close to the Warren River—and no explanation is given as to why the object was falling from the sky with no known origin.

In a second report, from April 7, 1966, in Bradford (inland and in the southwest), a witness described seeing a "saucer-shaped object about the size of a silver dollar." Equipped with three blinking red lights, it appeared at about 10 degrees elevation to the east. The witness, described only as a "student," watched it for about 10 minutes through a telescope; it was stationary at first then slowly ascended south along the horizon.

As is the case with many Project Blue Book reports, this was deemed a traditional aircraft sighting, as the area "is constantly traversed by civilian and military aircraft"—indeed, flying shapes of all types and sizes that the witness would no doubt have constantly seen. Still, there was something undoubtedly different about this aircraft, warranting the report.

The third report is, if nothing else, the most emphatic. At 11:04 p.m. on August 12, 1965, in Providence, a witness reported seeing two objects flying "one behind the other" from east-southeast to west-northwest. Seen through a telescope with 120 power, they flew at an altitude of about 7,000 feet, and each had five lights of bright yellow. "Behind the lights I could make out a gray shadow in a shape of a disc; all of the lights were connected to this body," the witness, whose name is blacked out throughout the report, writes in two pages of cursive script. "There were no engine sounds from them from the time we first saw them until we lost sight of them. I say 'we' because there were four other people who saw them besides myself."

The writer goes on to say that he has been a student of astronomy for eight years, "and I am pretty sure I can tell a plane or a meteorite or a satellite when I see one, and I'm positive that these objects were none of them."

The writer concludes that he queried the local Air National Guard, airport, and the Quonset Point Naval Air Station, and "none of them had any flights in the air at the time of our sighting."

The writer finishes with this quipping blow: "I'm writing this letter in the hopes that it might change your view on flying saucers and you'll do a little bit more than sit behind a desk and say that all these sightings are planets and stars."

The conclusion? "No data presented to indicate that the observation could NOT BE attributed to Aircraft."

Yes—but of what kind?

MYSTERIES ABOUND

Meanwhile, there are a few hundred reports from Rhode Island in the National UFO Reporting Center database (as well as on a handful of other witness reporting websites). These go as far back as the 1940s and include a whole host of phenomena, from fleeting, seconds-long sightings to far more intimate experiences.

One spectacular encounter of the third kind was relayed by a carpenter while on a job in South Kingstown: In July 1944 his father was in his workshop cellar when he claimed that a basketball-sized ball of light simply drifted in through the open cellar door. It "slowly traverse[d] . . . each wall, stopping at the workbench . . . then [sent] out 'electric sparks' to the tools while the father backed away in amazement." Silent and giving off no noticeable heat, the ball then slowly moved away and exited the way it had come in.

Similarly eerie—and unexplained—was a run-in that purportedly occurred in August 1971 at Quonset Point Air National Guard Station. While helping clean up after an outdoor cookout, a recently sworn-in Air Force second lieutenant working as a waiter spotted what he could only describe as a "being" that was human-like—but clearly gave off the aura of being anything but. Walking away at a moderate pace, it was between five and five and a half feet tall, thin "but not skinny," and without any distinctive coloring. Down to the clean, streamlined, one-piece suit that it wore—devoid of cuffs, seams, pockets, or closures—"everything was pale gray or dull silver," the witness wrote. It had no hair and wore no helmet or head covering and appeared to have human-like features. Seemingly nonchalantly, it strode across a well-lit field and disappeared into the surrounding reeds.

"I did not mention this to anyone at the time, as I didn't want anyone to think I was looney," the observer admitted. "The whole thing is still very vivid in my mind."

Numerous other sightings involve bright white or colored lights moving in straight lines, formations, or zigzagging around one another; beams of light seemingly emanating from nowhere; motionless balls hanging in the sky; kite-, teardrop-, chevron-, manta-, "backslash", and triangle-shaped objects; fiery cylinders; reflective objects; fireballs in a range of colors; stars dancing and moving like no celestial body is known to; unidentifiable strobes; hovering spheres.

AMONG THE CASE FILES

June 1956, Quonset Point: Airmen driving away from the base on a dark and barren road around 1:00 a.m. were transfixed by a long row of saucer-shaped lights hovering above the tree line. The lights stretched far into the darkness. As the men got out to look—struck by the absolute silence—they noticed a perfectly parallel row of lights farther away along the tree line. They then spotted a "huge and very wide" beam of light running through the forest below and between the two illuminated rows. As they watched, the pairs of lights across from each other touched the lower beam in tandem, then rose straight up and disappeared. This continued with each set, like a choreographed light show. When the men returned and reported to their base commander, they were told they had witnessed the phenomenon of the Northern Lights. However, aurora are extremely rare as far south as Rhode Island, and the men "stand by what they saw."

November 1958, Greenville: At a home near 21 West Approach Terrace Drive (adjacent to Slack Reservoir), a giant, looming object obscured about 70 percent of the sky to the southwest. It was described as "glowing silvery-white" and "shaped like two dinner plates top to top" with a narrow, glowing yellow-green band at its center. As it slowly rotated in the sky, five smaller, round objects zoomed in from radial directions and seamlessly merged with the larger craft. "There was absolutely no sound at all during the entire episode," the observer writes, offering a note on his credibility and intelligence by saying that, "at the time of the incident, I had already built an analog computer, radio equipment, and my own telescope."

"I firmly believe that we witnessed a UFO mother ship and five scouts."

July 1965, Port Judith: A Coast Guard watchman reported a "golden egg" chased by Navy fighters. "It was yellowish gold and was holding steady. It glowed, and I could not see the shape clearly, as the light of the object made the edges diffuse but strong."

—⁓—

September 1966, Coventry: Teenagers parked on a remote dirt road suddenly spotted a "very round and shiny object" in the dark sky. It resembled surgical steel and had a flat top and bottom. They watched as it ascended into the air, using successive beams of light to effectively push itself off the ground. Then it "jolt[ed] faster than we could keep our eyes on it, with no noise whatsoever."

—⁓—

November 1968, Exeter: On a rural road with no streetlights or nearby house lights, an observer described a "flying isosceles triangle with three lights." The lights in each corner were yellow, red, and "what seemed to be orange," and there was no light visible at the center of the craft. "The lights never flicked or wicked out, and the colors were constant," the witness recalled.

—⁓—

June 1979, Connecticut–Rhode Island border (Bristol County): When getting out of their car to watch a peculiar, moving red sphere in the sky—described as bright and about the size of a small fingernail—an "enormous" silent object suddenly appeared directly overhead, casting a bright red glow over the entire area. The male witness estimated it at 100 feet in diameter and, when he craned his neck to look up at it, recalled three silver-toned spoke-like features reflecting the red glow. He later wrote that the underside reminded him of an "automobile steering wheel," while he couldn't tell if the spokes were pointed upward or downward. In any case, it was "fascinating" and flicked away as suddenly as it had appeared.

January 1974, Pawtucket: While taking out the trash at around 10:00 p.m., a teenage boy and his friend were alerted by his younger sister. Her cries grew more frantic, and when they finally paid heed, they saw a craft hovering about 100 yards overhead. He described it as 16 feet in diameter, with reddish-pink flashing lights and a blinding central strobe; it seemed to pan up and down and inspect the earthlings as it hung above the roof of the three-door garage. Then it "made a letter 'Z' formation and shot out of sight into the night sky with a 'whoosh' sound with such velocity that no jet plane till today could achieve . . . leaving behind a trail of two fluorescent-green laser-like lights with a red and white light ray . . . that slowly dissolved in the air."

May 1976, Coventry: A woman stopped at a stoplight noticed a peculiar light about 100 feet away. "Instantly" it became three lights, which seemed to dance around one another. "The 'dance' seemed to be well choreographed," the viewer writes. "One red light was stationary in a center position, while two lights maneuvered up, down, around, behind, and in front of the center light." The two dancing lights then merged with the central one and with, "no sudden taking off, no streaking of lights [it was] just POOF, gone."

January 1977, Coventry: Upon seeing an "odd, bright, six-pointed light hovering over the trees in the distance" through their home's sliding glass windows, alarmed witnesses flashed on outside floodlights. This seemed to prompt a reaction: The points of light converged into a flat linear shape, accelerating toward the house. It then hovered—soundlessly—about 300 feet above. The observer estimated that it was at least 1,000 feet wide, with "enormous, cavernous bays beneath" but no light and no signs of movement inside. Afraid, the viewer admitted to hiding behind the window curtains—and upon looking back a minute or so later, the craft was gone. "There were no traces, no noises, nothing. It simply had disappeared."

—◦—

July 1980, traveling from Charlestown to Westerly: Two young-sters in the backseat of a car saw two objects appear out of nowhere, moving about 200 to 300 feet above the ground. They first dismissed them as planes, but upon closer examination, "they were silver discs almost, like, aluminum foil color" and appeared to be lit up from the inside. The writer reports that they came from the direction of the naval base in Newport, and she claims to still see them to this day on occasion—always three, flying very close together, "bobbing up and down, real high, and far away." The wit-ness adds in her entry that "I truly question if something is going on at the navy base in Newport."

—◦—

July 1983, Warwick: Several witnesses saw a large, metallic disc-shaped object hovering over a field along Warwick Avenue. The witness pulled his car over, as did three or four other drivers, to get a better look. The object was described as about 75 feet long and 25 feet high and hanging about 20 feet off the ground. It moved north before disappearing. Concurrently, the viewer saw an "errat-ically" moving object high up in the sky, "moving in directions like nothing we had then, or now."

Christmas Eve 1987, Exeter: At a home along State Route 102, a nine-year-old carrying presents out to a car looked up to see a "rectangular shaped UFO." It had white, red, and green lights, and the witness swore he saw "shadowy heads" in its white-lit windows. Moving in a straight line, the object suddenly "turned on a dime in an "L"-shaped line." The witness ran into the house to get his mother, and the two returned outside to see "the tail end of a flash" as the object quickly took off.

October 1990, Burlingame State Park, Charlestown: Two visitors to the park got what they described as a "close pass" of a "small, seemingly living object" illuminated in their headlights. The being or object approached from the 10 o'clock position, sweeping through the upper reach of the headlight beams and proceeding above the road and vehicle before rising into the forest. Both the driver and passenger had an "extremely clear and close view" and agreed that it was not a flying squirrel or other known local creature and "did not appear to be mechanical in any sense, but rather living material or possibly a living form itself." "Both of us felt we were in the presence of a highly aware and seemingly social object," the observer, identifying himself as an electronics engineering technician, recalled. He writes in reverence that it had a "general shape and grace of a manta [ray]" and seemed to possess other attributes of deep-sea animals, as well, including a circular area at its center with a subtle pattern of lines that radiated a "distinct and clearly visible internal glow." Its rounded wingtips also had a slight recurve. "I have no explanation for what we saw," the observer concluded.

June 1993, Block Island: Three housekeepers spotted a light due south and midway from the horizon that seemed to pulsate and change colors. "Red, blue, green, and white," the witness claimed. The light was "vaguely triangular" with an "orange translucence" and was accompanied by a "buzzing or humming." Going outside, the housekeepers were surprised to see the same pulsating light due north and found that they were surrounded by at least a dozen jellyfish-like objects that were "orange and hazy," "hovering, bouncing."

January 1997, East Greenwich: A driver spotted a UFO that was circular in shape, with "three distinct prolusion units" at its bottom and several red rectangular lights around its perimeter. It was described as traveling in straight lines and forming a triangular pattern, moving at an approximate airspeed of 150 miles an hour. The witness adds, "I believe that I was in some kind of mental contact with the occupants of the craft . . . as the triangular course seemed to circle directly around me."

TWENTY-FIRST CENTURY MYSTERIES

In recent years, as we have previously discussed, sightings have decreased—who can say why for sure? —compared to the heyday of traditional flying saucers, little green men, and Roswell conspiracies. Yet they indeed persist, with strange objects seen, felt, and sometimes even found.

In August 2017, for example, local residents and officials in Westerly removed an odd, unidentified object from East Beach. It was first spotted several months earlier, sticking out of the surf, repeatedly covered and uncovered by the tide and shifting sands. According to the *Providence Journal*, several dozen people gathered to watch on a sunny, windswept day as excavators worked to extract the object. They weren't able to remove it intact, instead bringing it up and out in all manner of "twisted and bent pieces," as the *Journal* described, "a metal strip here, a rod there," then attempted to reassemble it on the beach. When all its parts were available and arranged, the "thing" appeared to measure about six feet in diameter and six or seven feet tall, with a central axis, circular base, and eight steel legs or poles "radiating down and angling out."

Its pieces were then cleared away, loaded in a truck, and removed to an "undisclosed location," according to officials.

Lookers-on, one of whom held up a handwritten "I love aliens" sign as the media snapped pictures, commented that it appeared to be more like "landing gear" than something you'd see come off a boat. Peter Brockmann, president of the East Beach Association who arranged its removal, said he consulted with scientists at the University of Rhode Island and surmised that it may have been an acoustic device used to measure currents; after being deployed offshore, it detached and washed up on the beach.

"Or," he told the *Journal*, "maybe some little green guy will come lay claim to it."

Since the strange object hasn't been positively identified and there wasn't any further reported analysis of it, its fate—and origins—remain a mystery.

CASE FILES CONTINUED—HIGH-TECH TIMES, HIGH-TECH ENCOUNTERS

June 2000, Providence: A pilot flying on an instrument flight rules (IFR) plan at 8,000 feet mean sea level spotted what he first thought was a bird directly in his flight path, appearing to be "writhing in effort to avoid my plane (this is not an uncommon sight)." However, as it drew closer, he saw that it was an egg-shaped object standing on end, with its top and bottom each spiked with three distinct points. It had no lights, appeared to be moving in an eastbound direction, and passed "very close to and above" the right wing of the aircraft. The pilot immediately contacted air traffic control, which corroborated the object as a stationary "primary target" with no transponder or verifiable altitude information, trailing the plane by about a mile.

⸺ ⸻

November 2004, Newport: A witness writes that he received a kind of intense mental message to get up, retrieve his binoculars, and lie under the night sky. After some initial frustration at seeing only shooting stars, the witness writes that he observed two saucer-shaped craft at about 30,000 feet, "huge," with lights "emanating out from the edges." Then, suddenly, a "totally silent black triangle" appeared about 500 feet away in the viewer's field. On a successive night, the writer claims to have seen another craft, a "huge silent triangle with orange plasma round lights on each corner," gliding about 200 feet up and rotating at about 20 miles an hour. It then flew directly overhead, turned 90 degrees, and flew off.

⸺ ⸻

December 2005, Warwick: Around midnight, an observer saw a "strange (and very large) white plasma-like light on the horizon" that was shaped like a cigar. The observer estimated that it was 300 to 600 feet in length, and it moved from the left to right of their field of vision in a "nonlinear way"—that is, it appeared to skip or teleport forward. After about 5 or 10 minutes, the object stopped moving, and the viewer describes multiple tiny orange/red spheres being released from its top/center. Several of them proceeded to move through the woods, and "they appeared to be searching for something or just gathering info." One flew within about 250 feet of the viewer's home, offering a closer look at what seemed to be a "boxy sphere," metallic, 10 to 20 feet in diameter, with multiple red and orange lights. It made no noise; the witness describes it as simply floating slowly by, rotating "in random directions." After about a half-hour, the smaller objects finally made their way back to the larger object, reentering through the top, and the giant plasma light continued to move along until it was out of sight. The following morning, the witness writes, the sky was covered in many more chemical trails and "crisscross streaks" than the person had ever seen, then or since.

━━━◆━━━

June 2007, Narragansett: A motorcyclist traveling south on US Highway 1A noticed an object flying "very low and slow" to his left along the shoreline. Its wings were lit with "a very odd amber-tinged white light," and it had an "intense, flashing" white strobe light underneath it. As it moved along and he viewed it from behind, the viewer was "stunned" to see three oblong lighted areas that were a subdued lime green. "These lights, plus the odd gliding way the craft moved, convinced me that it was a UFO," he writes. "The craft was far too big, too low, and too slow to be anything conventional."

━━━◆━━━

February 2008, Middletown: At around 6:30 p.m., a mother and daughter saw a distinct spinning object with "big bright white lights." It "went to the right, and with a flash it was gone." The writer marvels, "I never thought this would happen to us."

May 2010, South Kingstown: A witness reported a small gray cylinder that was "perfectly stationary," situated at a higher altitude than a jet. Against a "very clear sky" with "excellent visibility," it slowly began to move north, accelerating, then inexplicably changed color from gray to white, then became opaque, and finally invisible. "I had the feeling that it knew I was watching it," the witness wrote.

February 2011, North Kingstown: A man sitting in his car described the shock of three bright flashes illuminating the ground around his vehicle. He emphasized their intensity, describing them as like "lightning flashes."

January 2014, West Greenwich (MUFON "Case 53853"): A couple traveling in a car on the highway captured five images of two hovering objects—"they were circular and had no lights," reported the female observer. In the photos, the objects appear as tiny specs above a tree line (presumably) blurred by movement. The couple got off at the next exit and drove toward the area where they believed they saw the objects. However, in that short period, "we had lost them in the trees . . . and by the time we reached the area they were previously above, they were gone," the witness writes.

July 2014, Westerly: A husband and wife enjoying a boat ride on a local lake suddenly looked up to see five to six "shiny chrome egg-shaped objects" hovering "perfectly still" at a height "about 50 percent lower than what a commercial aircraft would be flying at," the male witness reported. He then described how one of the crafts made a "hook type" move around one of the others "at a speed that no man-made craft could possibly do," before the objects began moving at a crawling speed across the daytime sky before disappearing.

———

September 2015, Westerly: A witness provided a concise report of "hundreds of thousands of tiny white, shimmery dots converging into clusters and going up into the sky." It lasted about 10 minutes, he wrote, emphasizing that they were "definitely not Chinese lanterns or insects."

———

September 2015, Block Island: Swimmers described a "pink, circular object floating through the air" at about 40 degrees above the horizon; it then zigzagged, dropped straight down, and disappeared.

———

July 2016, South Kingstown: In a particularly rare phenomenon, a witness was awoken by his dog's barking to be hit with a "very strong smell of something sweet and 'heavy' in the air," unlike anything he had experienced in his "60-plus years." He wrote that the smell made him dizzy and nauseous, and it seemed to come from everywhere and nowhere all at once. He looked up and all around, but there was nothing to accompany the smell or account for it. "I read that sometimes UFOs have been associated with smells or drifting silk-like substances," he explains in his entry, before concluding that the smell and the sensation dissipated after about 10 minutes.

August 2016, Providence: An observer out in the garden with his dog in the early-morning hours looked up to see a fast-moving, bright red orb. As he watched, it suddenly stopped and hovered, providing a clear view. It was "very distinct in shape and [had] no gas trail or anything surrounding it or following it when it moved," the observer wrote. The orb then proceeded to move rapidly right to left and back again, while changing colors from bright red to bright white, then intense red once more. The witness called to his wife, who he described as "very smart" and "professional," in a "high position with her company for several years." She also saw it and said she had never seen anything like it in her life, he recalled. The husband, meanwhile, marveled that "I myself have never seen anything move as fast, and then stop so quickly." He described how it moved from a "standstill, just hovering, to zipping . . . then stopping like it hit a wall."

October 2016, Wakefield: A woman watching the "blood moon" reported that it was suddenly blacked out and replaced by a sparkler or lightning-like phenomenon. Then a bright orange, "molten" object appeared, circular and about 75 percent the size of the moon. Moving back and forth to the north and south, it shone multiple lights toward the ground as if surveying the area. It also seemed to hum, the witness reported.

November 2016, Seekonk: Driving on Interstate 95 east toward the Massachusetts town of Fall River, an observer spotted a white, circular-shaped object flying about 300 feet or so above his vehicle. It seemed to be moving about 200 miles an hour, flying straight and then across his line of vision. "There was no noise, no exhaust smoke, no fire, no glowing," he wrote.

—◦—

July 2018, Warwick: A man out grilling in his backyard on a late afternoon that had "sunny, blue skies [and was] 80 degrees," caught a glimpse of three orange balls of light. "These things weren't like paper lanterns," he recalled. "These suckers were big," easily 50 feet in diameter, he estimated, making their way slowly across the sky 300 or so feet above his head. "No sound, perfectly quiet, and they had this majestic, almost stately, quality about them," he wrote. The only thing he could think to do? Take off his oven mitt and salute them.

—◦—

October 2018, Tiverton: An observer described a huge diamond-shaped craft with bright, unwavering, unblinking lights on both sides. It hovered over the trees for about four minutes, subtly jerked forward, then took off over the house, lights simply seeming to blink out.

And what of you Rhode Islanders who happen to be reading this? What peculiarities have you spotted in the ether?

Sources

Websites/Internet

The Allagash Incident, allagashufotwins.com

The Bennington Triangle, benningtontriangle.com

The Black Vault, theblackvault.com

Celebrate Boston, celebrateboston.com/ufo/first-ufo-sighting.htm; celebrateboston.com/ufo/new-haven-ufo-1647.htm; celebrateboston.com/ufo/first-uso-sighting.htm

Damned Connecticut, damnedct.com

Exeter UFO Festival, exeterufofestival.org

Fold3 by Ancestry (Project Blue Book files), fold3.com/title/461/project-blue-book-ufo-investigations#overview

HOWL Magazine, howlmag.com

Maine Vacations, etravelmaine.com/attractions/strange-maine/maine-ufo-sightings

Mutual UFO Network, mufon.com

National Investigations Committee on Aerial Phenomena, nicap.org

National UFO Reporting Center, nuforc.org

Near-Death Experiences and the Afterlife, www.near-death.com/experiences/triggers/alien-abduction.html

Pararational, pararational.com

Springfield Vermont News, springfieldvt.blogspot.com

Strange Maine, strangemaine.blogspot.com

UFO Casebook, ufocasebook.com

UFO Network Blog, ufo.net

UFOs at Close Sight, ufologie.patrickgross.org

UFO Odds, casino.org/ufo-odds

UFOs Northwest, ufosnw.com
UFO Stalker, ufostalker.com
The Vintage News, thevintagenews.com

Newspaper/Web-Based Articles

Berry, Michael. "UFOs in New Hampshire." *New Hampshire Magazine*, September 2015.

Bills, Joe. "Aliens in New England? A Timeline of UFO Sightings and Unusual Encounters." *New England Today Living*, August 1, 2018.

Blumenthal, Ralph. "Alien Nation: Have Humans Been Abducted by Extraterrestrials?" *Vanity Fair*, May 10, 2013.

Bolles, Dan. "Does Vermont Have Its Own Version of the Bermuda Triangle?" SevenDaysVT.com, October 26, 2016.

Breen, Tom. "The Truth Is Out There (in the Berkshires)." *Journal Inquirer*, May 23, 2018.

Burdy, Tom. "UFOs over Northern Maine—The 1975 Loring UFO Incident." StrangeNewEngland.com, June 26, 2015.

Byrne, Matt. "Unafraid of Alienating Themselves." *Portland Press Herald*, September 7, 2013.

Cooper, Helene, Ralph Blumenthal, and Leslie Kean. "Glowing Auras and 'Black Money': The Pentagon's Mysterious U.F.O. Program." *New York Times*, December 16, 2017.

Duckler, Ray. "Once upon a Time, Betty and Barney Hill Told a Story That Was Out of This World." *Concord Monitor*, March 17, 2018.

Encarnacao, Jack. "'Unbearable' Smell in Quincy a Mystery." *Patriot Ledger*, May 9, 2013.

Forte, Daniela. "The Mystery of the 'UFO' or Meteorite That Fell into Bantam Lake May Never Be Solved." *Litchfield County Times*, April 27, 2012.

Fraga, Brian. "Odd Airborne Lights Spark UFO Talk in SouthCoast." *SouthCoastToday*, December 6, 2011.

Gill-Austern, Maggie. "Flying Object Spooks Man." *Lewiston Sun Journal*, November 11, 2006.

———. "Odd Lights, Low Sounds Cause Stir." *Lewiston Sun Journal*, February 14, 2007.

SOURCES

Gunderson, Matt. "Unearthing the Truth of UFOs." *Boston Globe*, March 2, 2008.

Hampton, Daniel. "The States with Most UFO Sightings and Why They Have So Many." Patch.com, June 11, 2018.

Hartley, Ethan. "Witness Recalls Beverly UFO Sighting 50 Years Later." *Wicked Local Beverly*, April 22, 2016.

Heller, Paul. "March 1966: What Was in the Sky over Central Vermont?" *Barre Montpelier Times Argus*, September 3, 2013.

Imbrogno, Philip J. "Close Encounter on Interstate 84." May 31, 1993. http://theshadowlands.net/inter84.txt.

Kuffner, Alex. "The Day the Beach Stood Still: Westerly Object Removed." *Providence Journal*, August 31, 2017.

Lacina, Linda. "The First Alien-Abduction Account Described a Medical Exam with a Crude Pregnancy Test." History.com, September 4, 2018.

Lent, Colleen. "Exeter's UFO Kid Dead at 55." SeacoastOnline, March 2, 2003 (updated December 17, 2010).

Marsh, Roger. "Maine Witness Describes Close Encounter with Triangle UFO." OpenMinds.TV, April 10, 2017.

———. "Rhode Island Couple Photographs Hovering Black Disc UFOs." *Huffington Post*, February 3, 2014.

Ofgang, Erik. "CT Files: Connecticut's Real-Life Flying Saucer." *Connecticut Magazine*, July 5, 2017.

Palpini, Kristin. "Sheffield Orders New Landing Spot for UFO Monument." *Berkshire Eagle*, April 10, 2018.

Potila, Jessica. "Subject of 1976 UFO Casts Doubt on 'Allagash Abductions.'" *FiddleHead Focus*, September 10, 2016.

Preuss, Andreas. "Mysterious Metallic Object Uncovered on Rhode Island Beach." CNN.com, September 1, 2017.

Reilly, Adam. "Western Mass. Debates a UFO Monument—and How to Commemorate the Inexplicable." WGBH, May 31, 2018.

Rosenberg, Eli. "Former Navy Pilot Describes UFO Encounter Studied by Secret Pentagon Program." *Washington Post*, December 18, 2017.

Schinella, Tony. "Did You See the UFO on Sunday?" Patch.com, October 6, 2014.

———. "More UFO Lights Seen over Concord." Patch.com, September 24, 2015.

———. "Sketches of Nashua UFO Released." Patch.com, October 8, 2014.

———. "UFO Update: Craft Was Seen in Concord, Boscawen." Patch.com, November 26, 2014.

Shields, Bill. "Mystery Aircraft Frightens Quincy Residents." CBS Boston, May 9, 2013.

Smith, Margaret. "Investigators to Probe UFO Reported over Mass. Town." *Herald News*, March 2, 2012.

———. "UFO Reported over Chelmsford." *Wicked Local Chelmsford*, April 17, 2018.

Sottile, Alexis. "Geek Road Trip: New Hampshire's Massive UFO Festival." *SYFY Wire*, September 18, 2018.

Speigel, Lee. "Boomerang UFO Zigzags over NH." *Huffington Post*, November 25, 2014.

———. "UFOs over Massachusetts Not Easy for Air Force to Explain Away." *Huffington Post*, January 25, 2013.

Stevens, Wendelle. "UFO Pictures from Rhode Island in 1967." Open-Minds.TV, July 19, 2010.

Vike, Brian. "Loring AFB UFO Incident—Ex-Military Serviceman Speaks." April 12, 2006. rense.com/general70/speaks.htm.

———. "The Loring AFB UFO Incident—A Son Relating His Father's Story." October 17, 2006. rense.com/general73/lroing.htm.

Ward, Kent. "The Loring UFO Episode Revisited." *Bangor Daily News*, October 2, 2009.

Webb, Walter N. "Encounter at Buff Ledge." 1994. hyper.net/ufo/txt/buff-ledge.txt.

Weber, Tom. "Allagash Abductees Still Wonder What Happened." *Bangor Daily News*, July 25, 1998.

Whittington, Mark. "The Amazing Connecticut UFO Close Encounter in 1987." *Top Secret Writers*, February 5, 2018.

Books

Hughes, Patricia. *More Lost Loot: Ghostly New England Treasure Tales.* Atglen, PA: Schiffer, 2011.

Slevik, Nomar. *UFOs over Maine: Close Encounters from the Pine Tree State.* Atglen, PA: Schiffer, 2014.

ABOUT THE AUTHOR

Taryn Plumb is a freelance writer based outside of Portland, Maine, whose subjects range from ghosts and goblins to the intricacies of finance (which subject frightens you more?). She has a fascination with the paranormal and is also the author of *Haunted Boston* and *Haunted Maine Lighthouses*.